PRESIDENT'S MALARIA INITIATIVE

Malawi

Malaria Operational Plan FY 2016

TABLE OF CONTENTS

ABBREVIATIONS and ACRONYMS

ACT	Artemisinin-based combination therapy
AL	Artemether-lumefantrine
ANC	Antenatal care
ASAQ	Artesunate-amodiaquine
BCC	Behavior change communication
CDC	Centers for Disease Control and Prevention
CHAM	Christian Health Association of Malawi
CMED	Central Monitoring and Evaluation Department
CMST	Central Medical Stores Trust
DFID	United Kingdom Department for International Development
DHS	Demographic and Health Survey
DHIS 2	District health information system
DP	Dihydroartemisin-piperaquine
EHP	Essential Health Package
EPI	Expanded Program on Immunization
FANC	Focused antenatal care
FY	Fiscal year
GHI	Global Health Initiative
Global Fund	Global Fund to Fight AIDS, Tuberculosis and Malaria
GoM	Government of Malawi
HMIS	Health Management Information System
HSA	Health surveillance assistants
HSSP	Health Sector Strategic Plan
HTSS	Health Technical Support Services
iCCM	Integrated community case management
IEC	Information, education, communication
IMCI	Integrated management of childhood illness
IPTp	Intermittent preventive treatment in pregnant women
IRS	Indoor residual spraying
ITN	Insecticide treated net
IVM	Integrated vector management
LMIS	Logistics management information system
M&E	Monitoring and evaluation
MICS	Multiple indicator cluster study
MIP	Malaria in pregnancy
MIS	Malaria indicator survey
MOH	Ministry of Health
NFM	New Funding Model
MOP	Malaria Operational Plan
NMCP	National Malaria Control Program
OTSS	Outreach training and supportive supervision
PEPFAR	President's Emergency Plan for AIDS Relief
PBO	Piperonyl butoxide
PMI	President's Malaria Initiative

RBM	Roll Back Malaria
RDT	Rapid diagnostic test
SP	Sulfadoxine-pyrimethamine
SPA	Service provision assessment
SSDI	Support for Service Delivery Integration
SWAp	Health sector-wide approach
TES	Therapeutic efficacy study
TWG	Technical working group
UNICEF	United Nations Children's Fund
USAID	United States Agency for International Development
USG	United States Government
VHC	Village health clinics
WHO	World Health Organization

I. EXECUTIVE SUMMARY

When it was launched in 2005, the goal of the President's Malaria Initiative (PMI) was to reduce malaria-related mortality by 50% across 15 high-burden countries in sub-Saharan Africa through a rapid scale-up of four proven and highly effective malaria prevention and treatment measures: insecticide-treated mosquito nets (ITNs); indoor residual spraying (IRS); accurate diagnosis and prompt treatment with artemisinin-based combination therapies (ACTs); and intermittent preventive treatment of pregnant women (IPTp). With the passage of the Tom Lantos and Henry J. Hyde Global Leadership against HIV/AIDS, Tuberculosis, and Malaria Act in 2008, PMI developed a U.S. Government Malaria Strategy for 2009–2014. This strategy included a long-term vision for malaria control in which sustained high coverage with malaria prevention and treatment interventions would progressively lead to malaria-free zones in Africa, with the ultimate goal of worldwide malaria eradication by 2040-2050. Consistent with this strategy and the increase in annual appropriations supporting PMI, four new sub-Saharan African countries and one regional program in the Greater Mekong Subregion of Southeast Asia were added in 2011. The contributions of PMI, together with those of other partners, have led to dramatic improvements in the coverage of malaria control interventions in PMI-supported countries, and all 15 original countries have documented substantial declines in all-cause mortality rates among children less than five years of age.

In 2015, PMI launched the next six-year strategy, setting forth a bold and ambitious goal and objectives. The PMI Strategy 2015-2020 takes into account the progress over the past decade and the new challenges that have arisen. Malaria prevention and control remains a major U.S. foreign assistance objective and PMI's Strategy fully aligns with the U.S. Government's vision of ending preventable child and maternal deaths and ending extreme poverty. It is also in line with the goals articulated in the RBM Partnership's second generation global malaria action plan, *Action and Investment to defeat Malaria (AIM) 2016-2030: for a Malaria-Free World* and WHO's updated *Global Technical Strategy: 2016-2030*. Under the PMI Strategy 2015-2020, the U.S. Government's goal is to work with PMI-supported countries and partners to further reduce malaria deaths and substantially decrease malaria morbidity, towards the long-term goal of elimination.

Malawi was selected as a PMI focus country in FY 2006.

This FY 2016 Malaria Operational Plan presents a detailed implementation plan for Malawi, based on the strategies of PMI and the National Malaria Control Program (NMCP). It was developed in consultation with the NMCP and with the participation of national and international partners involved in malaria prevention and control in the country. The activities that PMI is proposing to support fit in well with the National Malaria Control strategy and plan and build on investments made by PMI and other partners to improve and expand malaria-related services, including the Global Fund to Fight AIDS, Tuberculosis, and Malaria (Global Fund) malaria grants. This document briefly reviews the current status of malaria control policies and interventions in Malawi, describes progress to date, identifies challenges and unmet needs to achieving the targets of the NMCP and PMI, and provides a description of activities that are planned with FY 2016 funding.

The proposed FY 2016 PMI budget for Malawi is $22 million. PMI will support the following intervention areas with these funds:

Insecticide-treated nets (ITNs): The NMCP developed the Malawi Vector Control Strategy 2015-2019 and implementation plan, in which the distribution and promotion of ITN use are the primary malaria prevention interventions in the country. PMI has consistently supported NMCP efforts through the procurement and distribution of ITNs for continuous distribution to pregnant women and children under the age of one year at antenatal care clinics and delivery or expanded program on immunization visits. Over the past five years, an estimated 6 million ITNs have been distributed countrywide in Malawi through routine channels. In addition, PMI has supported Malawi with technical support for planning and management of routine and mass distribution mechanisms, as well as support for behavior change communication and community mobilization efforts to improve the uptake and utilization of ITNs.

With FY 2016 funding, PMI will continue to support the NMCP's efforts to ensure high coverage of pregnant women and children through the procurement and distribution of ITNs through routine channels (800,000 ITNs), and support training and supervision of health workers on ITN distribution. PMI will also provide continued support for ITN durability monitoring following the planned 2015 mass campaign. Behavior change communication (BCC) activities will continue to be supported through national-level communication and the community-based small grants program that promote ITN use among all household members and enhance net care and repair.

Indoor residual spraying (IRS): The 2011-2016 Malawi Malaria Strategic Plan incorporates IRS as part of an integrated vector management strategy. Depending on available resources, the plan proposes resuming IRS with long-acting organophosphates in three high-burden districts in 2016, with the goal of expanding to eight high transmission districts.

In 2007, PMI piloted IRS with a pyrethroid insecticide in part of one high transmission district in Malawi, eventually scaling up to cover two districts. In 2010, the Government of Malawi (GoM) began supporting IRS in an additional five districts in 2010. However, high levels of pyrethroid and carbamate resistance in *An. funestus* necessitated a shift to organophosphate insecticides. Given the high cost and short duration of residual efficacy of short-acting organophosphate, the only alternative available at the time, PMI suspended direct support for IRS in Malawi after the 2011 spray season.

Although the future of the IRS program is uncertain due to resource challenges, the GoM currently plans to resume spraying and has indicated that they will procure insecticide and fund the operational expenses of the campaign. NMCP has requested technical assistance from PMI to ensure that the campaign is implemented in a timely and effective manner and in compliance with accepted environmental and worker safety standards. Therefore, with FY 2016 funding, PMI plans to fund activities to catalyze the IRS campaign, including support for microplanning, geocoding, training, environmental compliance, worker safety, and other logistical activities. Furthermore, PMI will continue to support entomological monitoring in targeted districts.

Malaria in pregnancy (MIP): Through focused antenatal care (FANC), PMI supports all aspects the Ministry of Health's three-pronged approach to reducing the burden of malaria in pregnancy: use of intermittent preventive treatment in pregnant women (IPTp) during antenatal care (ANC), distribution of ITNs to pregnant women, and effective case management of malarial illness and anemia. PMI, in conjunction with the NMCP and Reproductive Health Directorate, has worked to increase uptake of IPTp through training and supervision of providers and assistance with directly observed treatment. With support from PMI, the Ministry of Health (MOH) updated the national policy on IPTp to reflect the new World Health Organization (WHO) guidelines, and trained nearly all health workers in these new guidelines in 2014-15. The revised policy removes previous barriers to IPTp uptake, under which women were only to receive IPTp at specific intervals during pregnancy. Nevertheless, despite two decades of IPTp policy in Malawi, coverage goals have yet to be met. There are still systemic barriers to seeking ANC in the first trimester andnd increasing sulfadoxine-pyrimethamine (SP) resistance represents another significant threat to IPTp in Malawi.

With FY 2016 funding, PMI will continue integrated and malaria-specific behavior change communication activities in support of IPTp, case management, and ITN use at national and community levels; provide free ITNs for routine distribution at ANC visits and at labor and delivery for newborns; procure sulfadoxine-pyrimethamine (2 million treatments) and supplies to ensure directly observed therapy and IPTp uptake at ANC; support supervision activities for malaria in pregnancy interventions as part of the focused antenatal care package; and help improve the collection of data on IPTp through support to strengthen the Health Management Information System (HMIS) system.

Case management: Increasing capacity to ensure prompt and effective case management and reduce the presumptive use of antimalarial medications is a key priority in Malawi's Malaria Strategic Plan. PMI has supported the Government of Malawi through procurement of malaria commodities including rapid diagnostic tests (RDTs), artemisinin-based combination therapy (ACT) treatments, injectable artesunate, and artesunate suppositories; training of health facility workers; outreach training and supportive supervision (OTSS) to laboratory and clinical supervisors; and support to village health clinics.

Supply chain issues continue to be a key concern in Malawi. Due to issues of leakage and general mismanagement, a parallel supply chain was created in 2010 to distribute donor-procured malaria commodities. In 2012, representatives from the GoM, Central Medical Stores Trust (CMST), and partners, including World Health Organization, the Global Fund, DFID, and PMI, conducted a review of the supply chain management system and developed a *Joint Strategy for Supply Chain Integration in Malawi*. In addition to support for Central Medical Store (CMS) reform, the USG has supported efforts to improve the overall supply chain through continued support to the MOH to strengthen planning and coordination centrally and improve commodity management and reporting at the district and facility levels.

Consumption trends for ACTs have continued to increase over the past two years, from roughly 9 million ACTs in 2013, to 10.5 million ACTs in 2014. In the same period, reported malaria cases have also increased, but the substantial gap between ACT consumption and reported cases has continued to widen; in 2014, 6 million cases were reported through the national HMIS.

Given this large discrepancy, PMI supported a rapid assessment of case reporting and ACT consumption in November 2014. Findings indicate several drivers for the high and increasing consumption, including: poor case reporting through the HMIS, presumptive treatment, lack of provider compliance with RDT results, widespread use of ACTs without confirmation at the community level, stock mismanagement, inadequate storage space for commodities, and theft of commodities at the facility and perhaps community level. Furthermore, a lack of legal enforcement creates an enabling environment for continued theft. Working with NMCP and other partners, PMI has developed an action plan to improve commodity oversight and management – including improved supervision at the district, facility and community levels, better use of data for decision making, and audits of facilities with discrepancies between consumption and reported cases. Additionally, the recent training of health workers in malaria case management included an emphasis on compliance with RDTs and appropriate use of ACTs, which, when coupled with appropriate follow up and supervision, should improve provider behavior.

With FY 2016 funding, PMI will focus on improving community and facility-based case management services in ten priority districts, those with the highest malaria burden in the country. Case management commodities, specifically RDTs and ACTs, will still be supplied nationwide. PMI will support training of health surveillance assistants in the use of RDTs and pre-referral use of rectal artesunate in order to expand diagnostic and treatment capabilities in the community. Follow-up supervisory visits will assess effectiveness of case management trainings and identify areas needing further attention. PMI will continue to support and expand a core group of microscopy trainers to improve the quality of microscopy services. In order to further enhance microscopy capabilities, a national archive of malaria slides is being created with PMI support. In addition, PMI funding will target BCC interventions focused on appropriate care seeking behavior and medication adherence for both uncomplicated and severe malaria at the community level. With regard to pharmaceutical management, PMI will continue to provide technical assistance to GoM to improve management, oversight, and accountability for supply chain and logistics management and also maintain support for the parallel PMI supply chain management system.

Health systems strengthening and capacity building: PMI supports a broad array of health system strengthening activities which cut across intervention areas, such as training of health workers, supply chain management and health information systems strengthening, drug quality monitoring, and NMCP capacity building. Through its implementing partners, PMI provides technical support to the MOH to help improve policies, management and leadership, and fiscal responsibility. PMI promotes evidence-based policies, strengthens the management and technical capacity of the NMCP and other MOH divisions, supports development and strengthening of electronic data systems, strengthens the zonal supervision structures, bolsters decentralized management of health services at the district level, and strengthens the government's capacity for financial planning and management and budget execution.

With FY 2016 funding, PMI Malawi plans to focus and concentrate its service delivery strengthening efforts in ten high malaria burden districts, building government capacity for facility-based case management, FANC and delivery of IPTp, community mobilization and integrated community case management (iCCM), and monitoring and evaluation at the district level. These capacity building efforts will include training and expanded supportive supervision and mentoring to relevant cadres (e.g., facility and community health care workers, pharmacy technicians and assistants, etc.). Simultaneously, at the central level, PMI will provide technical and operational support to the NMCP and other key parts of the MOH (such as Central Monitoring and Evaluation Department (CMED) and Integrated Management of Childhood Illness Unit), support policy development and dissemination, strengthen pharmaceutical supply chain management, and reinforce the HMIS and monitoring and evaluation.

Behavior change communication (BCC): The NMCP put in place a Malaria Communication Strategy (2011–2015), whose goal is to improve behavioral change interventions through advocacy and social mobilization, and has established a technical committee to support and guide the implementation of this strategy. PMI Malawi's BCC efforts are in line with the National Strategy and support an integrated approach focused on ITNs, MIP, and case management. BCC activities have included national campaigns and door-to-door visits to promote year-round ITN use; large-scale campaigns to emphasize ANC attendance to improve IPTp uptake; and community-based campaigns that emphasize ITN utilization, as well as improved case management through the promotion of early care-seeking behavior. BCC strategies have been employed from the national to the community level to target policy makers, health care providers, and community members. In promoting malaria interventions, PMI has utilized a variety of BCC approaches, including educational meetings, mass media, print media, community drama, and interpersonal communication activities.

With FY 2016 funding, PMI plans to support an integrated BCC approach at the national level and at the community level in ten focus districts with ITN, IPTp, and case management messaging. National level efforts will focus on advocacy, mass media communication, and materials development, while community level efforts will focus on interpersonal and small group interventions.

Monitoring and evaluation (M&E): The NMCP's 2011-2016 Malaria Strategic Plan calls for strengthening of surveillance, monitoring and evaluation systems through routine health management information systems, malaria-specific surveillance and special surveys to gather entomologic, epidemiologic, and coverage indicator data. PMI has supported numerous monitoring and evaluation activities in Malawi, including household surveys (Demographic Health Survey [DHS], Malaria Indicator Survey [MIS]), health facility surveys (service provision assessment, end-use verification survey), malaria surveillance and routine system support (sentinel surveillance, HMIS), therapeutic efficacy studies, and entomological surveillance and resistance monitoring.

With FY 2016 funding, PMI plans to continue to support strengthening of routine health management information systems and malaria-specific surveillance and special surveys to gather entomologic, epidemiologic, and coverage indicator data. PMI will also provide continued support for ITN durability monitoring following the 2015 mass campaign.

Operational research (OR): The NMCP's 2011-2015 Malaria Strategic Plan calls for strengthening operational research through the support of local capacity building and the creation of stronger coordination between NMCP and researchers to harmonize and prioritize operational research efforts. PMI-funded operational research has provided important data for decision-making, including studies measuring the durability of long-lasting ITNs, the impact of IRS, the effectiveness of the IPTp strategy, the quality of health facility case management practices for uncomplicated and severe malaria, the ability of patients to complete recommended first-line treatment for malaria, the distribution of potentially drug-resistant parasites and mosquitoes and the effectiveness of ITNs in an area with significant pyrethroid resistance.

In early 2015, a PMI-funded evaluation of mobile-telephone text messaging to improve health worker performance was initiated. End-line surveys are planned for the November 2015 and May 2016 to assess the impact of the intervention. In 2015, PMI will continue to monitor the levels of SP resistance and will support a repeat evaluation of the effectiveness of IPTp focusing on the effect of the sextuple (dhps581) mutation, which is associated with extremely high levels of resistance. In addition, PMI has been supporting the NMCP to develop a research agenda and data dissemination platform to better coordinate and share research among partners in Malawi.

With FY 2016 funds, the research focus will be to complete the cell phone messaging evaluation, and continue a study to assess the efficacy of IPTp with dihydroartemisin-piperaquine (DP) compared to SP, as well as to initiate an evaluation of the effect of community delivery of IPTp-SP on IPTp uptake and ANC attendance.

II. STRATEGY

1. Introduction

When it was launched in 2005, the goal of PMI was to reduce malaria-related mortality by 50% across 15 high-burden countries in sub-Saharan Africa through a rapid scale-up of four proven and highly effective malaria prevention and treatment measures: insecticide-treated mosquito nets (ITNs); indoor residual spraying (IRS); accurate diagnosis and prompt treatment with artemisinin-based combination therapies (ACTs); and intermittent preventive treatment of pregnant women (IPTp). With the passage of the Tom Lantos and Henry J. Hyde Global Leadership against HIV/AIDS, Tuberculosis, and Malaria Act in 2008, PMI developed a U.S. Government Malaria Strategy for 2009–2014. This strategy included a long-term vision for malaria control in which sustained high coverage with malaria prevention and treatment interventions would progressively lead to malaria-free zones in Africa, with the ultimate goal of worldwide malaria eradication by 2040-2050. Consistent with this strategy and the increase in annual appropriations supporting PMI, four new sub-Saharan African countries and one regional program in the Greater Mekong Subregion of Southeast Asia were added in 2011. The contributions of PMI, together with those of other partners, have led to dramatic improvements in the coverage of malaria control interventions in PMI-supported countries, and all 15 original countries have documented substantial declines in all-cause mortality rates among children less than five years of age.

In 2015, PMI launched the next six-year strategy, setting forth a bold and ambitious goal and objectives. The PMI Strategy 2015-2020 takes into account the progress over the past decade and the new challenges that have arisen. Malaria prevention and control remains a major U.S. foreign assistance objective and PMI's Strategy fully aligns with the U.S. Government's vision of ending preventable child and maternal deaths and ending extreme poverty. It is also in line with the goals articulated in the RBM Partnership's second generation global malaria action plan, *Action and Investment to defeat Malaria (AIM) 2016-2030: for a Malaria-Free World* and WHO's updated *Global Technical Strategy: 2016-2030*. Under the PMI Strategy 2015-2020, the U.S. Government's goal is to work with PMI-supported countries and partners to further reduce malaria deaths and substantially decrease malaria morbidity, towards the long-term goal of elimination.

Malawi was selected as a PMI focus country in FY 2006.

This FY 2016 Malaria Operational Plan presents a detailed implementation plan for Malawi, based on the strategies of PMI and the National Malaria Control Program's (NMCP) 2011 – 2016 Malaria Strategic Plan. It was developed in consultation with the NMCP and with the participation of national and international partners involved in malaria prevention and control in the country. The activities that PMI is proposing to support fit in well with the National Malaria Control strategy and plan and build on investments made by PMI and other partners to improve and expand malaria-related services, including the Global Fund to Fight AIDS, Tuberculosis, and Malaria (Global Fund) malaria grants. This document briefly reviews the current status of malaria control policies and interventions in Malawi, describes progress to date, identifies challenges and unmet needs to achieving the targets of the NMCP and PMI, and provides a description of activities that are planned with FY 2016 funding.

2. Malaria situation in Malawi

Malawi is a landlocked country bordered by Tanzania to the north, Zambia to the west, and Mozambique to the east and south. The population in 2016 is projected to be 16.8 million, comprised of approximately 51 percent women and approximately 20 percent children under five years of age (National Statistical Office of Malawi). Rapid population growth continues to be a challenge, with an average of 5 children per woman (2014 Multiple Indicator Clustor Survey [MICS]) and an annual population growth rate of 2.9 percent, thus the proportion of children less than five years old continues to grow.

Malaria is endemic in more than 95 percent of the country (Figure 1). Transmission is perennial in most parts of the country and peaks after the start of the annual rains that typically begin in November and last through April. The highest transmission areas are found along the hotter, wetter, and more humid low-lying areas (lakeshore, Shire River Valley, and central plain), while the lowest risk areas fall along the highlands of Rumphi, Mzimba, Chitipa, and Kirk Range.[1] *Anopheles funestus* is considered to be the primary vector species; *An. gambiae* s.s. and *An. arabiensis* also are present and may predominate in some areas at certain times of the year. *Plasmodium falciparum* is the most common species of malaria, accounting for 98 percent of the infections and all severe disease and deaths.

---

[1] Kazembe LN1, Kleinschmidt I, Holtz TH, Sharp BL. 2006. *Spatial analysis and mapping of malaria risk in Malawi using point-referenced prevalence of infection data.* Int J Health Geogr. 2006 Sep 20;5:41.

Figure 1: Predicted population-weighted *Plasmodium falciparum* parasite prevalence in children two to ten years of age, Malawi 2010-2012[2,3]

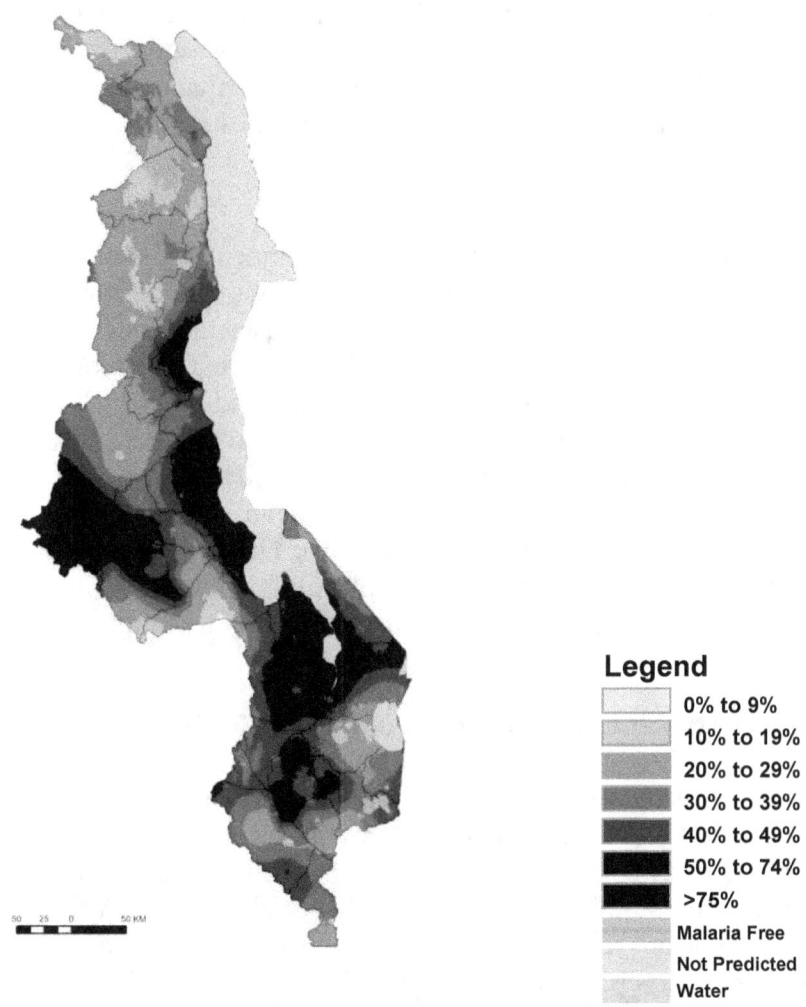

Legend

	0% to 9%
	10% to 19%
	20% to 29%
	30% to 39%
	40% to 49%
	50% to 74%
	>75%
	Malaria Free
	Not Predicted
	Water

Malaria continues to be a major public health problem and is responsible for approximately 6.2[4] million presumed and confirmed cases reported annually from health facilities and by the community case management program, and 36 percent of all outpatient visits across all ages (2014 Health Management Information System [HMIS] data, unpublished). Among children under five years, malaria parasite prevalence by microscopy was 33 percent nationally (2014 MIS).

---

[2] Okiro EA, Noor AM, Malinga J, Mitto B, Mundia CW, Mathanga D, Mzilahowa T, Snow RW (2014). *An epidemiological profile of malaria and its control in Malawi*. A report prepared for the Ministry of Health, the Roll Back Malaria Partnership and the Department for International Development, UK. March, 2014.

[3] Electronic and manual searches for published and unpublished reports were used to identify available malaria prevalence surveys (including the 2010 and 2012 Malawi Malaria Indicator Surveys). Age-corrected survey data (sample size and numbers positive) at known locations (longitude and latitude) and times (year) with a minimal set of conservative, long-term climate and human settlement covariates were used. Covariates statistically significant to the age-corrected infection prevalence were identified (in this case urbanization). Empirical data and spatially matched covariates were used within a Bayesian hierarchical space–time model to produce continuous maps of $PfPR_{2-10}$ for 2010-2012.

[4] According to NMCP reports, there were 5 million cases reported from facilities (a combination of parasitologically confirmed and presumed) and 1.2 million case reported from iCCM (all which are presumed).

Pregnant women and their fetuses are at high risk of the negative consequences of malaria. From 1996-2007, the incidence of placental malaria fell from 25 percent to 7 percent at the main referral hospital in Blantyre.[5] Although this is a selected population with unusually easy access to the best medical services available in the public sector in Malawi, a similar low level of acute placental malaria (5 percent) was measured in a rural area in Machinga District that was evaluated as part of a study monitoring the continued effectiveness of sulfadoxine-pyrimethamine (SP).[6]

Over the past five years, PMI-supported entomological monitoring has documented increasing vector insecticide resistance, including the rise and spread of pyrethroid and carbamate resistance in *An. funestus*, which is the primary vector species in Malawi. Pyrethroid resistance in *An. funestus* was first identified in 2010-2011 and recent data from 2014 demonstrated low mortality (2 to 14 percent for deltamethrin, 3 to 57 percent for permethrin). Pyrethroid and piperonyl butoxide (PBO) synergist bioassays conducted in Nkhotakota and Chikwawa districts showed a significant increase in mortality, indicating that pyrethroid resistance is partially mediated by mixed-function oxidases. Resistance to carbamate insecticides was first documented in 2011 and data from 2014 showed mortality rates as low as 4 to 6 percent in two districts. All *An. funestus* populations that tested against the organophosphates malathion and pirimiphos-methyl have been fully susceptible, while populations tested against DDT have been classified as susceptible or suspected resistant.

3. Country health system delivery structure and Ministry of Health (MOH) organization

The Malawi health service delivery system is pyramidal, consisting of tertiary, secondary, primary, and community care levels. District and central hospitals provide secondary and tertiary care services, respectively, but also provide primary care to individuals within their catchment area. Primary care is delivered through clinics and health centers where curative, maternity, and preventive services are offered. Access to health facilities is limited: approximately half of Malawians live within a five-kilometer radius percent of a health facility. In response, Malawi has more than 3,500 health surveillance assistants (HSAs) in hard-to-reach areas who provide integrated community case management (iCCM) in addition to other services through village health clinics (VHCs). HSAs are trained to assess, classify, and provide first-line treatment for selected childhood illnesses, including malaria, in addition to referral to the next level of care. Local community-based organizations also provide non-clinical malaria services such as behavior change communication (BCC) on key malaria messages, counseling, and net distribution. The Malawi health system is highly decentralized with many programming decisions made at the district level and coordination and supervision done by the zonal level (there are five zones). The Christian Health Association of Malawi (CHAM) operates health facilities mainly in rural areas nationwide and provides approximately one-third of health

---

[5] Feng G, Simpson JA, Chaluluka E, Molyneux ME, Rogerson SJ. 2010. *Decreasing burden of malaria in pregnancy in Malawian women and its relationship to use of intermittent preventive therapy or bed nets.* PLoS One. 2010 Aug 6;5(8):e12012.

[6] Gutman J, Mwandama D, Wiegand RE, Ali D, Mathanga DP, Skarbinski J. 2013. *Effectiveness of intermittent preventive treatment with sulfadoxine-pyrimethamine during pregnancy on maternal and birth outcomes in Machinga district, Malawi.* J Infect Dis. 2013 Sep;208(6):907-16.

services; fees are charged for the Essential Health Package (EHP) where service level agreements with the government have not been established.

The NMCP is located under the Ministry of Health's (MOH) Directorate of Preventive Health Services. The NMCP Program Manager is thus the Deputy Director of Preventive Health Services. In recent years, the program has expanded and now incorporates a core group of 12 technical officers. The NMCP sets policies, establishes strategies, coordinates activities, and provides technical guidance for the MOH with respect to malaria prevention and control interventions. The management structure is comprised of 29 District Malaria Coordinators to direct activities in each district, as well as 29 District ITN Coordinators. Currently, these positions are filled by staff members with other primary designations, but plans are underway to convert the District Malaria Coordinator positions to full-time. Other staff at the district level, including the District Health Officer, District Pharmacist, and District HMIS Officer, are critical to the malaria program.

4. National malaria control strategy

The 2011-2016 National Malaria Strategic Plan, entitled "Towards Universal Coverage," builds on the successes achieved and lessons learned during implementation of the previous two strategic plans. The current Malaria Strategic Plan was developed and approved by the MOH in early 2011 and originally covered the period 2011-2015. The NMCP conducted a mid-term review in 2014 and extended the plan to cover 2016, in line with the Malawi Health Sector Strategic Plan (HSSP). Within the Malaria Strategic Plan, Malawi aims to move from targeted malaria control interventions to provision of universal access to proven interventions so that all Malawians at risk of malaria have equitable access to malaria prevention, care and treatment. The NMCP activities are designed to be implemented within the HSSP and the health sector-wide approach (SWAp), including the provision of the essential health package. Specifically, the Malaria Strategic Plan objectives aim to ensure that by 2016 the MOH is in a position to:

- Achieve universal coverage of all interventions with an 80 percent or higher utilization rate of proven malaria interventions;
- Strengthen the systems for surveillance, M&E, and operational research to better track implementation of malaria control activities and provide the information necessary for effective programmatic decision-making; and
- Strengthen capacity in program management to achieve malaria program objectives at all levels of health service delivery.

Within the Malaria Strategic Plan, six primary intervention areas are targeted: integrated vector management (IVM); case management; malaria in pregnancy; social mobilization and advocacy; surveillance, monitoring, evaluation and operations research; and program management.

IVM: The NMCP ITN policy promotes free distribution of ITNs for children born in health facilities, children attending their first visit under the Expanded Program on Immunization (EPI) (if an ITN was not received at birth), and to pregnant women at their first visit to an antenatal care (ANC) clinic. The policy also supports time-limited, national, free distribution campaigns that are conducted every two to three years. Malawi aims to achieve universal coverage with ITNs, defined as one net for every two people, with the objective of increasing net ownership and net usage among pregnant women and children under 5 years of age to at least 90 percent by 2016.

Within the Malaria Strategic Plan, Malawi intends to expand IRS to up to eight highly endemic districts by 2015. However, since the mid-term review in 2014, the NMCP has developed and adopted an evidence-based IVM strategy to guide future vector control activities and entomologic monitoring. An implementation plan for this strategy is currently under development. Given the emergence and expansion of pyrethroid and carbamate resistance, the high cost of alternative insecticides, and the limited funding from the Government of Malawi (GoM), the IVM implementation plan will likely call for a more limited and targeted expansion of IRS.

Although ITN distribution and IRS remain the main malaria vector control interventions in Malawi, larval source management will be used as a complementary strategy, as resources from GoM and other donors allow.

Case management: The primary focus of the Malaria Strategic Plan includes improvement of parasitological confirmation of malaria through the use of microscopy in central and district hospitals, as well as in facilities with high patient loads, and the use of rapid diagnostic tests (RDTs) at all levels of the health system. The phased roll-out of RDTs to health facilities has been completed. The roll out to the community level has met with considerable delays and is now planned for 2015.

The Malaria Strategic Plan also calls for strengthening of the systems for quality assurance for both diagnosis and treatment. In addition, health worker capacity for patient care as well as post-marketing surveillance and pharmacovigilance will be strengthened.

In 2006, the MOH selected artemether-lumefantrine (AL) as the first-line and artesunate-amodiaquine (ASAQ) as the second-line treatment for uncomplicated malaria, reserving parenteral quinine for the treatment of severe malaria and oral quinine for the management of malaria in the first trimester of pregnancy. In 2013, the MOH revised the guidelines for the management of severe malaria to recommend treatment with parenteral artesunate at health facility and hospital levels and rectal artesunate as pre-referral treatment at community level. The MOH has completed training for health workers in the use of parenteral artesunate and the roll-out of this medication is underway. The NMCP plans to commence the roll out of rectal artesunate as part of the roll out of RDTs to the community level.

Malaria in pregnancy: As part of a comprehensive focused ANC (FANC) package, Malawi is committed to increasing the provision of SP in all health facilities. The national policy on IPTp has been revised to be in line with WHO guidance and Malawi is finalizing guidelines and training manuals for the implementation of the policy.

Social mobilization and advocacy: The Malaria Strategic Plan and the 2009-2014 Malaria Communication Strategy recommend social mobilization and advocacy strategies to increase the use of all malaria interventions through increased efforts aimed at qualitative and quantitative research, prioritization for promotion of targeted positive behaviors, and capacity building. PMI has supported NMCP efforts to update the Malaria Communication Plan to be temporally in line with the 2011-2016 HSSP. The target for finalization and dissemination of this plan is the end of calendar year 2015.

Surveillance, monitoring and evaluation, and operations research: The Malaria Strategic Plan aims to strengthen routine data systems, surveillance, and operations research, promoting use of information while strengthening capacities for data use at all levels. The NMCP will continue to work closely with the Central Monitoring and Evaluation Department (CMED) and other partners to incorporate appropriate malaria indicators into the district health information system (DHIS 2) and strengthen the overall HMIS. The 2011-2015 Monitoring and Evaluation Plan outlines the key strategic areas and focuses on tracking progress and measuring results of the various malaria prevention and control interventions to better inform policy, planning, and decision making. A revision of the Monitoring and Evaluation Plan is scheduled for calendar year 2015.

Program management: The Malaria Strategic Plan also emphasizes capacity strengthening in program management at all levels of health service delivery. This requires resource mobilization and strengthened coordination across partners. The NMCP has linked its management objectives to existing national and international development strategies to enhance its policy direction. The procurement and supply chain management system was highlighted as an area requiring significant strengthening.

5. Updates in the strategy section

There have been four developments in the past 12 months that should be noted:

- The NMCP has finalized the mid-term review of the 2011-2015 Malaria Strategic Plan and a revised version has been disseminated. Revisions were made to the strategic objectives; however, the primary interventions and approaches remain unchanged. The timeline for the plan has been extended until 2016 to align with the Malawi 2011-2016 HSSP.
- With technical support from PMI and other malaria and iCCM stakeholders, Malawi submitted a combined malaria and iCCM concept note for the Global Fund New Funding Model (NFM) in January 2015. The concept note has been reviewed and endorsed by the Global Fund Technical Review Panel and Grants Approval Committee and is now in the grant-making stage. If successfully negotiated, the grant will include approximately $26 million of within allocation funding, primarily for procurement of ACTs, RDTs, and parenteral artesunate and for iCCM strengthening. An additional $6 million of above allocation funding is targeted mainly to strengthening BCC and M&E. This funding is critical to the successful implementation of malaria prevention and control activities in Malawi and delays in grant making and disbursement could result in stockouts of life-saving malaria commodities.
- With FY 2013 funding, PMI provided partial support and technical assistance to the third MIS in Malawi. The 2014 MIS was conducted during May-June 2014 and final results were disseminated in March 2015. A second MICS was also conducted during the first half of 2014 with support from UNICEF. At time of writing, the key findings have been released, but the full report is still pending. Please see *Strategy: Progress on indicators to date* for a summary of results from these national household surveys.

- PMI's primary service delivery, systems strengthening, and communications implementing partners will be ceasing operations at the end of FY 2015. The PMI team is currently working with USAID Mission staff to design the subsequent project for these critical programmatic areas. As part of the new design, PMI intends to reduce the number of targeted districts from the current 15 districts (not selected based on malaria-specific criteria) to 10 of the highest burden malaria districts. These districts have been chosen primarily based on the available epidemiologic data from the HMIS and models of district level prevalence from anemia and parasitemia studies. The PMI team anticipates that this more epidemiologically-driven and focused approach will increase the impact of the limited PMI funding on overall malaria transmission.

6. Integration, collaboration, and coordination

In Malawi, the MOH and donors developed the health SWAp under the HSSP to coordinate donor and GoM activities. Under the SWAp, resources are given either to a common pool or to projects aligned with GoM strategies and plans, as is PMI's approach. The SWAp is governed by a secretariat supported by technical working groups that provide technical guidance and decision-making on key technical issues. Development partners also participate in the SWAp governance structures through the Health Donor Group; PMI is represented in this group by the Director of USAID's Office of Health, Population, and Nutrition (HPN).

Malaria-specific partners
PMI actively coordinates with development partners in Malawi on malaria and cross-cutting health issues. For malaria-specific activities, the Global Fund is the other key development partner. To date, Malawi has received a total of approximately $167 million for malaria activities from the Global Fund and significant additional funding is still committed within the Round 9 and Transitional Funding Model grants. The MOH submitted a concept note under the NFM in January 2015 and has received initial approval from the Global Fund Technical Review Panel for an additional approximately $32 million for malaria for January 2016 through December 2017. The majority of resources (over $21 million) under the NFM grant will be used for malaria commodities and distribution, with additional resources for iCCM, BCC, M&E, and program management. Under the NFM, Malawi will have two principle recipients: MOH for commodities and World Vision for programmatic activities. At the time of writing, grant making negotiations for the NFM are underway and there may be minor shifts in the funding amounts for each area.

The NMCP receives additional technical assistance from a number of partners:

- The United Nations Children's Fund (UNICEF) supports programmatic management, as well as malaria prevention and control efforts at the district level, including the procurement of ACTs for community case management (CCM), and development of BCC materials.
- The World Health Organization (WHO) provides assistance on a variety of technical issues.
- The Clinton Health Access Initiative (CHAI) promotes the use of injectable artesunate as the first-line treatment for severe malaria and serves as the in-country implementer of the

UNITAID grant to Medicines for Malaria Venture to purchase injectable artesunate. CHAI also provides technical support to the NMCP on commodity quantification and Global Fund issues.

- Save the Children, with support from the WHO Global Malaria Programme and the Government of Canada, implements the Rapid Access Expansion (RAcE) program to support the scale-up of integrated community case management (iCCM) in seven districts.

Other relevant health partners

In addition to malaria, the United States Government (USG) in Malawi supports a robust health program with emphasis on HIV/AIDS; maternal, newborn, and child health; family planning; nutrition; water, sanitation, and hygiene; and health systems strengthening. Malawi is a President's Emergency Plan for AIDS Relief (PEPFAR) long-term strategy country, receiving over $100 million in FY 2015 including significant increases over the past two years, for care and treatment of HIV, key population prevention, community based care and support and health systems strengthening. USAID HPN receives approximately $38 million for other health sectors in FY 2015 and supports service delivery improvements, community mobilization, and systems strengthening in focus districts, in addition to significant central level support. PEPFAR, USAID HPN, and PMI share several implementing partners working on integrated or common platforms to support improved health outcomes in Malawi. The PMI team works closely with PEPFAR and the USAID health teams to coordinate activities.

The United Kingdom Department for International Development (DFID) is a key partner in the broader health sector, with extensive focus on improving the health supply chain. In addition to procurement and distribution of essential medicines, DFID provides substantial technical assistance to the Central Medical Store Trust (CMST) and may provide additional support through USAID to roll out the pre-fabricated storage units to health centers in Malawi to improve the quality and security of commodity storage. DFID is also exploring additional opportunities to support the health sector at the district level, including strengthening community structures to improve commodity security and accountability.

7. PMI goal, objectives, strategic areas, and key indicators

Under the PMI Strategy for 2015-2020, the U.S. Government's goal is to work with PMI-supported countries and partners to further reduce malaria deaths and substantially decrease malaria morbidity, towards the long-term goal of elimination. Building upon the progress to date in PMI-supported countries, PMI will work with NMCPs and partners to accomplish the following objectives by 2020:

1. Reduce malaria mortality by one-third from 2015 levels in PMI-supported countries, achieving a greater than 80% reduction from PMI's original 2000 baseline levels.

2. Reduce malaria morbidity in PMI-supported countries by 40% from 2015 levels.

3. Assist at least five PMI-supported countries to meet the World Health Organization's (WHO) criteria for national or sub-national pre-elimination.[7]

These objectives will be accomplished by emphasizing five core areas of strategic focus:
1. Achieving and sustaining scale of proven interventions
2. Adapting to changing epidemiology and incorporating new tools
3. Improving countries' capacity to collect and use information
4. Mitigating risk against the current malaria control gains
5. Building capacity and health systems towards full country ownership

To track progress toward achieving and sustaining scale of proven interventions (area of strategic focus #1), PMI will continue to track the key indicators recommended by the Roll Back Malaria Monitoring and Evaluation Reference Group (RBM MERG) as listed below:

- Proportion of households with at least one ITN
- Proportion of households with at least one ITN for every two people
- Proportion of children under five years old who slept under an ITN the previous night
- Proportion of pregnant women who slept under an ITN the previous night
- Proportion of households in targeted districts protected by IRS
- Proportion of children under five years old with fever in the last two weeks for whom advice or treatment was sought
- Proportion of children under five with fever in the last two weeks who had a finger or heel stick
- Proportion receiving an ACT among children under five years old with fever in the last two weeks who received any antimalarial drugs
- Proportion of women who received two or more doses of IPTp for malaria during ANC visits during their last pregnancy

8. Progress on coverage/impact indicators to date

The 2006 MICS provides the baseline data for PMI's program. The most up-to-date information comes from the 2014 MIS.

---

[7] http://whqlibdoc.who.int/publications/2007/9789241596084_eng.pdf

Table 1: Evolution of Key Malaria Indicators in Malawi from 2006 to 2014

Indicator	2006 MICS	2010 MIS	2010 DHS	2012 MIS	2014 MICS	2014 MIS
% Households with at least one ITN	38	58	57	55	80	70
% Households with at least one ITN for every two people	N/A	N/A	N/A	19	34	30
% Children under five who slept under an ITN the previous night	25	55	38	56	65	67
% Pregnant women who slept under an ITN the previous night	8	49	35	51	61	62
% Children under five years old with fever in the last two weeks for whom advice or treatment was sought	N/A	26*	65	50	75	59
% Children under five with fever in the last two weeks who had a finger or heel stick	N/A	7	17	21	42	33
% Children receiving an ACT among children under five years old with fever in the last two weeks who received any antimalarial drugs	N/A	N/A	N/A	91	88	92
% Women who received two or more doses of IPTp during their last pregnancy in the last two years	48	60	55	54	N/A**	63

*The 2010 MIS collected data on care seeking within 24 hours of fever onset. The subsequent surveys, including the 2010 Demographic and Health Survey (DHS), did not specify a time frame.
** IPTp2 data was not released as part of the currently available key findings report.

9. Other relevant evidence on progress

PMI Malawi has supported two national health facility surveys to assess the status of case management of malaria in public health facilities. The first was conducted in 2011 (prior to the national roll-out of RDTs to health facilities) and focused on the management of uncomplicated malaria. In total, 107 health facilities, 2,019 outpatients, and 135 health workers were surveyed. Key findings include:

- Only 42 percent of patients attended facilities with functional microscopy. The quality of facility microscopy was poor compared to expert microscopists (sensitivity = 47 percent and specificity = 84 percent).
- Thirty-four percent of all patients seeking curative care at outpatient departments during the high-transmission season had parasitologically-confirmed, uncomplicated malaria.
- Sixty-seven percent of patients with malaria confirmed by microscopy were correctly treated with an ACT; 95 percent were correctly dosed. The main cause of incorrect treatment was malaria cases missed by clinicians.
- Thirty-one percent of patients without malaria received an ACT.
- Most patients were seen by health workers (69 percent) explicitly trained on the malaria treatment guidelines.

The second national health facility survey was conducted in 2012 and focused on the management of severe malaria. In total, 200 health workers were surveyed at 36 hospitals that admit patients with severe malaria and 1,252 inpatient records were reviewed. Key findings include:

- Forty-two percent of all patients were given an admission diagnosis of malaria.
- RDTs were available in 97 percent of the facilities, but were out of stock at least once in the prior three months in 44 percent of facilities. Microscopy supplies were available in 89 percent of the facilities, but were out of stock in 22 percent of facilities in the prior three months.
- Sixty-five percent of patients had parasitological confirmation of their diagnosis on admission.
- Quinine was available in 92 percent of the hospitals on the day of the survey, but 26 percent of facilities reported at least one stockout of all severe malaria treatments within the prior three months. Seventy-six percent of all severe malaria patients received intravenous quinine, the first-line medication (during the time of the survey) for the treatment of severe malaria.
- On the job malaria training was reported by 57 percent of health workers, primarily on the use of RDTs. Only 5 percent reported malaria supervision in the prior six months.
- Health workers cited availability of treatment (58 percent), availability of diagnostic supplies (32 percent), and knowledge gaps (30 percent) as the main obstacles to malaria care.

With funding and support from PMI, Malawi and the Roll Back Malaria (RBM) partnership completed an impact evaluation of malaria control efforts between 2000 and 2010. The *Progress and Impact Series* report was launched in April 2013. Key findings included a 41 percent reduction in under-five mortality from 188 to 112 deaths per 1000 live births over the period 1996-2000 and 2006-2010, and modeling, which estimated that approximately 21,600 deaths among children under five-years of age were prevented by malaria control interventions.

The 2013-14 service provision assessment (SPA) was designed to be a census of all formal sector health facilities in Malawi. The assessment used health facility inventory, health provider and client exit interview questionnaires, and observations protocols. Key findings include:

- Of all facilities, 96 percent offer malaria diagnosis and/or treatment services. Only 65 percent of facilities offer ANC services.
- Among all facilities offering malaria diagnosis and/or treatment, 61 percent had staff trained on malaria case management. First-line ACTs and RDTs were available in 92 percent and 88 percent of these facilities, respectively. Parenteral quinine for the treatment of severe malaria was available in 90 percent of facilities. Parenteral artesunate, which is being rolled out as the new first-line agent for severe malaria, was available in only 10 percent of facilities.
- Among facilities offering ANC services, 75 and 84 percent of hospitals and health centers, respectively, had ITNs available. SP for IPTp was available in 99 percent of these facilities.

10. Challenges and opportunities

Malawi's malaria program continues to face substantial challenges, including: 1) a limited overall funding envelope relative to the scale of the malaria-specific and overall health systems needs in Malawi; 2) delays in Global Fund disbursements for existing grants, related primarily to financial management issues within the GoM; 3) continued data system challenges for both routine disease surveillance and monitoring of commodity distribution and consumption, coupled with insufficient analysis and use of data for programmatic decision-making; 4) continued supply chain challenges 5) increasing insecticide resistance, which threatens the IRS program and potentially the ITN program; 6) SP resistance, which threatens the IPTp program; and 7) insufficient human resource capacity at all levels of the system.

Although transmission intensity varies geographically within Malawi, nearly the entire population of Malawi is at risk and even the districts with lowest estimated prevalence and incidence experience high disease burden (see Figure 1). Seasonal variation in transmission has been documented, with lower transmission during the drier months; however, even during these drier periods, significant malaria transmission occurs. Given this epidemiologic context and the limited health infrastructure and human resource capacity in Malawi, significant resources are required to make gains in malaria prevention and control. Collectively, PMI, the Global Fund, and other development partners provide substantial funding; however, contributions from the GoM remain limited given the financial problems faced by Malawi, and a large proportion of donor funding is targeted to ensuring large quantities of life-saving commodities are available. This leaves insufficient resources for prevention activities and capacity building within the malaria sector. In addition, considerable delays have occurred in the disbursement of Global Fund resources to Malawi in recent years, resulting in heavy reliance on PMI resources. Although this situation has improved following changes to the in-country monitoring and disbursement system by Global Fund, many critical activities have been significantly delayed; most notably, the planned 2015 ITN mass distribution campaign. Finally, delays in Malawi's submission of the NFM concept note have pushed back the timeline for additional Global Fund contributions. Recognizing that the resources available for prevention and capacity building activities are limited, PMI plans to focus and concentrate its resources by reducing the number of target districts under the new service delivery and systems strengthening projects. Please see *Operational Plan* for more details.

Routine monitoring of malaria indicators through the HMIS remains a challenge and poor data quality continues to limit the ability of the MOH to make evidenced-based programmatic decisions. Further, lack of integration of disease surveillance data (through HMIS) and commodity data (through logistics management information system, LMIS) makes it difficult to effectively distribute malaria commodities and ensure appropriate use accountability for commodities at the health facility level. Recently, the GoM has initiated efforts to improve the quality of health systems data and CMED has developed a strategy to improve the overall health information system. Under this strategy, DHIS 2 will become the central platform for all data collection by either direct entry or linkage to existing data systems. Efforts are currently underway to realize this strategy, including a stakeholder-driven process to streamline the core and program-specific indicators collected. PMI will provide continued technical support to this process and also explore opportunities to improve Malawi's capacity to analyze and use these data for decision-making at all levels of the health system.

Since PMI began work in Malawi, supply chain challenges have plagued the program. In mid-2010, PMI became aware of significant thefts of PMI-procured antimalarial drugs from the Central Medical Stores Trust (CMST), resulting in the withdrawal of USG-funded commodities from CMST and the establishment of a temporary parallel supply chain to service delivery points. Improved implementation of this parallel system has resulted in less frequent stockouts of antimalarial commodities. However, an outdated LMIS, irregular procurement and delivery of commodities, and a lack of dispensed-to-user data continue to limit the ability of this system to accurately forecast commodity needs and ensure availability of the commodities at the point of service. PMI has shared costs for this parallel supply chain with the Global Fund over the last several years. However, the Global Fund recently contracted a new distribution agent, which has resulted in two parallel supply chains for malaria and has increased the costs of the PMI supply chain mechanism. This creates the additional burden of managing distribution of malaria commodities across two separate partners, each with different timelines and structures.

Of particular concern related to malaria commodities, consumption of ACTs has increased dramatically over the past few years. Currently, consumption of ACTs is disproportionately higher than the number of cases reported through the HMIS, as well as the number of RDTs being used. Although continued presumptive treatment, changes in transmission intensity, and insufficient stock management and reporting may also be factors, repeated anecdotal reports suggest that commodity theft may play a significant role. This dramatically increased ACT consumption is extremely concerning and PMI is working with the USAID Mission, other partners, and the GoM to address this issue.

Vector control faces its own challenges, primarily related to the emergence and expansion of insecticide resistance to pyrethroids and carbamates. This caused the PMI-supported IRS program to change to a more expensive and short-acting organophosphate insecticide, which ultimately made the IRS program unsustainable within the PMI Malawi budget envelope. PMI has worked with the MOH and other partners to create a stakeholder-driven, evidenced-based

IVM strategy to determine the most appropriate way forward for Malawi's vector control efforts. An implementation plan for this strategy is under development and, if a viable way forward for IRS can be delineated, may provide an opportunity for further PMI investments in vector control. The impact of pyrethroid resistance on the effectiveness of ITNs is not clear; additional research is needed.

Results from studies in Malawi suggest increasing levels of SP resistance in the parasites infecting pregnant women and limited effects of IPTp-SP on birth outcomes. Given the current lack of a viable alternative to SP for IPTp, these findings represent a serious threat to the current and future effectiveness of the IPTp program in Malawi. PMI is actively supporting efforts to monitor SP resistance and identify potential alternative medications for IPTp.

Finally, Malawi continues to face major human resource capacity issues at all levels of the health system. The lack of sufficient numbers of qualified staff hampers efforts to implement malaria prevention and control interventions and has often resulted in a reliance upon health workers with lower levels of training for the performance of key activities (e.g., patient attendants conducting RDTs). Further, the relatively low wages for health workers and managers compared to other jobs requiring similar levels of training (e.g., in the private sector) incentivizes these workers to pursue activities that will supplement their wages, often taking health care workers away from their posts and duties. Finally, limited accountability for poor job performance, including the mismanagement and theft of commodities, makes it necessary for PMI and other development partners to invest significant resources, time, and energy into oversight of activities and for the maintenance of a parallel supply chain system for commodities. Although these human resource issues are beyond the scope of PMI to address alone, the PMI team is working with the U.S. Mission, other development partners, and the GoM to promote civil service reform within Malawi. This is a key objective of the U.S Mission in Malawi and the PMI team is hopeful that progress will be made in the coming years.

III. OPERATIONAL PLAN

PMI Support Strategy

PMI's strategy is to support the MOH and the NMCP to implement the Malaria Strategic Plan. While maintaining nationwide support for certain interventions (e.g., commodity procurement and distribution), PMI plans to adapt its strategy over the coming years to focus key interventions in ten of the districts with the highest malaria burden. Service delivery support, community mobilization, and district-level health systems strengthening activities are among those that will be prioritized in focus districts. The PMI team anticipates that this more epidemiologically-driven and focused approach will increase the impact of the limited PMI funding on overall malaria transmission. PMI will work closely with the MOH and other malaria partners to ensure PMI-funded activities in the focus districts are in-line with the priorities of the GoM, support national level initiatives, and are coordinated with the activities of other partners working in the non-focus districts.

PMI is committed to ensuring high net ownership and use by continuing to support the procurement and nationwide distribution of ITNs through routine systems at ANC and maternity clinics, in addition to providing logistical support for universal coverage campaigns. Following the universal coverage campaign in 2015, which will be funded primarily by the Global Fund, PMI will support durability monitoring of the ITNs distributed. PMI will explore other channels to provide ITNs on a continuous basis to provide more opportunities to increase the number of nets in each household.

Although PMI recognizes IRS as a key malaria prevention strategy, the documented pyrethroid resistance and high cost of alternative insecticides have made implementing an effective, affordable IRS program challenging. Following the development of IVM strategy and draft implementation plan, PMI intends to support planned GoM IRS activities in the coming years through technical support for microplanning, geocoding, training, environmental compliance, worker safety, and other logistical activities. These activities will be conducted in districts identified in the draft IVM implementation plan.

IPTp is one of the key interventions for reducing the impact of malaria in Malawi. In addition to strengthening IPTp services through ANC in 10 focus districts, PMI is monitoring *P. falciparum* resistance to SP, and the effect of the sextuple *dhfr/dhps* mutant among *P. falciparum* isolates from pregnant women in Malawi in response to evidence that SP is becoming less effective within the IPTp program. Biomarker monitoring for SP resistance will help to inform IPTp policy. PMI will also support an evaluation of alternative drugs which could replace SP for IPTp.

At the facility and community levels, PMI is committed to ensuring that there is access to high quality malaria case management. PMI will maintain support to the parallel supply chain to distribute ACTs, RDTs, and other commodities to all districts. At the central level, PMI will continue to provide technical assistance to improve the capacity of the CMST, introduce an improved electronic LMIS, strengthen NMCP and Health Technical Support Services (HTSS) ability to manage the multiple malaria supply chains, and improve the LMIS at the district level. In focus districts, PMI will continue to provide supportive supervision and follow-up training for the management of malaria as part of a broader maternal and child health effort. At the community level, PMI will work in the ten designated districts to support HSAs with training, oversight, and other support for iCCM services, counseling, and referral. PMI will continue to work with the NMCP to expand the iCCM program to include pre-referral rectal artesunate and RDTs. PMI will also continue to strengthen quality assurance for diagnostics, for both microscopy and RDTs, at the facility and community level in focus districts. Finally, PMI will place greater focus on supporting zonal and district structures to improve supervision and oversight of malaria interventions, including providing operational support to District Malaria Coordinators.

PMI will place renewed emphasis on improving use of commodity and health data for decision making, in response to the high and increasing number of ACTs used in the country, in comparison to the low numbers of malaria cases reported and number of RDTs used. Working through the district and zonal structures, PMI will support data reviews as well as efforts to engage community members and local governance structures to improve accountability for commodities.

All of these activities will be grounded in a strong monitoring and evaluation framework that includes population-based surveys, strengthening of HMIS data and other relevant activities. PMI will support the implementation of DHS every five years with an MIS survey in the intermediate years to determine progress against PMI and NMCP targets. This will be complemented by regular monitoring of HMIS data by the NMCP, commodity consumption data, entomological data, and other surveys such as health facility surveys and targeted operations research supported by PMI and other groups.

1. Insecticide-treated nets

NMCP/PMI objectives
The 2011-16 Malaria Strategic Plan calls for universal coverage with ITNs (defined as one net for every two individuals), and outlines specific targets to be reached by 2016, including ownership of at least one ITN by 90 percent of households and 90 percent ITN use among children less than five years of age and pregnant women. There are three main channels of ITN distribution in the country: 1) free routine distribution to pregnant women and children less than one year of age through ANC and EPI clinics,[8] 2) time-limited, intermittent distribution to the general population through mass campaigns, and 3) sale of subsidized ITNs through the private sector. Though not a formal distribution channel, the NMCP also distributes ITNs to affected populations during disasters, most notably flood disasters that have occurred each of the past three years. The NMCP, with technical and financial support from PMI, recently developed the Malawi Vector Control Strategy 2015-2019 and an associated implementation plan in which the distribution and promotion of ITN use are the primary malaria prevention interventions in the country.

Progress since PMI was launched
PMI has consistently supported NMCP efforts through the procurement and distribution of ITNs for continuous distribution to pregnant women and children under the age of one year. The ITN

---

[8] Following the 2012 mass distribution campaign, the NMCP shifted the target population for continuous ITN distribution from children less than five years of age to children less than one year of age. This change is reflected in the revised 2011-2106 Malaria Strategic Plan.

policy includes free distribution of ITNs for pregnant women at their first visit to an ANC clinic and for new babies in health facilities at delivery or at their first visit to an EPI clinic if an ITN was not received at birth. Over the past five years, an estimated 6 million ITNs have been distributed countrywide in Malawi through the routine channels. During the same period, PMI has supported Malawi with technical support for planning and management of routine and mass distribution mechanisms. In addition, PMI has funded behavior change communication and community mobilization efforts to improve the uptake and utilization of ITNs.

Malawi conducted its first nationwide mass distribution of free ITNs in 2012 with financial support provided primarily by the Global Fund. PMI procured and distributed ITNs for rural areas of Lilongwe District and provided technical assistance for overall campaign planning and operations. In total, 5.6 million ITNs were distributed by all partners.

Between 2010 and 2014, household ownership of at least one ITN had increased from 58 percent to 70 percent (MIS 2010, MIS 2014). Compared to the 2012 MIS, reported ITN utilization in the 2014 MIS has improved among children less than five years of age (from 56 percent to 67 percent) and pregnant women (from 51 percent to 62 percent). In households where at least one ITN was available, 87 percent of children less than five years old, 85 percent of pregnant women, and 72 percent of the general population slept under an ITN the night before the survey (MIS 2014). Among all age and risk groups, usage was higher in households owning at least one ITN, living in urban areas, and in the higher wealth quintile.

Progress during the last 12-18 months
In 2015, PMI funded the procurement and distribution of approximately 900,000 ITNs to pregnant women and children less than one year of age through the routine distribution system; an additional 400,000 routine ITNs were distributed with support from the Global Fund. PMI also provided technical assistance to the NMCP for ITN quantification and distribution planning, monitoring of ITN distribution through spot checks, supportive supervision of ANC and EPI staff, and the implementation of an online data collection system for distribution monitoring of ITNs. With support from the Global Fund and PMI, the NMCP conducted a 2014 MIS that assessed estimated access, ownership, and utilization of ITNs.

PMI continued to work with the NMCP to strengthen partnerships that exist between the NMCP and stakeholders around ITN procurement and distribution, including support for the quarterly meetings of the National Malaria Vector Control Sub-Technical Working Group. PMI continued to fund national mass media and print media campaigns to emphasize nightly ITN use by all household members, as well as proper care and repair of nets. In addition, PMI funded community-based organizations and local non-governmental organizations to increase awareness, promote correct and consistent use and proper care and repair.

In 2014, NMCP conducted a "mini-mass campaign" using ITNs that were originally intended for a mop-up campaign following the 2012 mass distribution to cover missed households. Funding delays resulted in the postponement of this mop-up effort and the decision was eventually made to distribute these nets in in the six districts that were among the first to receive ITNs in the 2012 mass campaign, and thus where it had been three years since a mass distribution. PMI funded the registration and verification activities for this effort, in which over 1.2 million ITNs were successfully distributed. This "mini-mass campaign" served as the first phase of a universal distribution campaign. The NMCP plans to distribute ITNs in the remaining districts in 2015 with operational support from Global Fund and Concern Universal. The PMI in-country team is providing significant direct technical assistance for campaign planning and implementation, in addition to funding for technical support by PMI's ITN distribution partner. This campaign is expected to distribute approximately 9 million ITNs and will target coverage by one ITN per sleeping space.

PMI supported the development of the Malawi Vector Control Strategy 2015-2019 and an associated implementation planto guide the MOH in the implementation of recommended and effective malaria vector control interventions in a sustainable and cost-effective manner. Among the vector control strategies highlighted in this strategy, ITNs are considered the highest priority intervention.

Commodity gap analysis

Table 2. ITN Gap Analysis

Calendar Year	2015	2016	2017
Total Targeted Population	16,310,430	16,783,432	17,270,152
Continuous Distribution Needs			
Channel #1: ANC*	815,522	841,645	868,578
Channel #2: Newborn (at EPI / Labor and Delivery)**	504,479	516,635	529,092
Estimated Total Need for Continuous	1,320,000	1,358,280	1,397,670
Mass Distribution Needs			
2015 mass distribution campaign			
Estimated Total Need for Campaigns	9,061,350	0	0
Total Calculated Need: Routine and Campaign	**10,381,350**	**1,358,280**	**1,397,670**
Partner Contributions			
ITNs carried over from previous year	0	0	49,220
ITNs from MOH	0	0	0
ITNs from Global Fund	9,481,350	0	0
ITNs from Other Donors	0	0	0
ITNs planned with PMI funding	900,000¥	1,407,500±	1,348,450†
Total ITNs Available	**10,381,350**	**1,407,500**	**1,397,670**
Total ITN Surplus (Gap)	**0**	**49,220**	**0**

* Number of pregnant women is estimated as 5% of the total population.
** Assume approximately 3% of total population receives an ITN at labor and delivery or EPI (a portion of all pregnant women).
¥ From FY 2013 resources.

 ± Includes 800,000 from FY 2014 and 607,500 from FY 2015.
 † Includes 607,500 nets from FY 2015 and 800,000 from FY 2016.

Plans and justification

PMI will continue to support the NMCP's efforts to ensure high coverage of pregnant women and children less than one year of age through the procurement and distribution of ITNs through routine channels, and support for the training and supervision of health workers on ITN distribution. PMI will also provide continued support for ITN durability monitoring following the planned 2015 mass campaign which will be initiated using prior year funding (please see the Monitoring and Evaluation section). BCC activities will continue to be supported through national-level communication and the community-based small grants program that promote ITN use among all household members and enhance net care and repair (please see BCC section).

Proposed activities with FY 2016 funding: **($3,656,000)**

- Procurement of 800,000 ITNs for distribution to pregnant women and children under one through routine channels (ANC and maternity clinics) ($2,856,000);

- Support management, oversight, and distribution of PMI-procured ITNs to health facilities for routine distribution. Includes customs clearing, warehousing, transport, distribution, and ITN tracking, as well as technical assistance to the NMCP for ITN quantification and distribution planning, monitoring of ITN distribution through spot checks, and supportive supervision of ANC and EPI staff ($800,000).

2. **Indoor residual spraying**

NMCP/PMI objectives

The 2011-2016 Malawi Malaria Strategic Plan incorporates IRS as part of an integrated vector management strategy, which also includes vector surveillance and insecticide resistance management, routine and mass distribution of ITNs, and larval source management in targeted areas. Depending on available resources, the plan calls for the implementation of IRS in at least three districts, with the goal of expanding to eight high transmission districts. With PMI support, the NMCP and vector control stakeholders developed an integrated Malaria Vector Control strategy in 2014. IRS activities in this strategy include: 1) strengthening policy and planning for IRS through needs assessments, timely forecasting, selection, and procurement of IRS commodities; 2) building capacity at national and district levels to implement IRS through improved training and supervision; 3) implementing BCC to increase household acceptance of IRS; 4) ensuring compliance with health and safety of personnel and environmental safeguards; 5) monitoring and evaluating IRS implementation; and 6) undertaking regular entomological monitoring and insecticide resistance surveillance to guide selection of insecticides for IRS and spray areas. NMCP and stakeholders are currently drafting an implementation plan for this strategy with PMI support.

Progress since PMI was launched

In 2007, PMI piloted IRS with a pyrethroid insecticide in a portion of one high transmission district in Malawi, eventually scaling up to cover two districts. Given the early success of the

PMI IRS program, the GoM began supporting IRS in an additional five districts in 2010, for a total of seven high-burden districts. However, high levels of pyrethroid and carbamate resistance in *An. funestus* (described below) necessitated a shift to organophosphate insecticides in the two PMI districts in 2010. At that time, only a short-acting organophosphate was available. Given the high cost and short duration of residual efficacy, PMI suspended direct support for IRS in Malawi after the 2011 spray season.

Following the cessation of PMI-funded IRS, the GoM continued to implement IRS using pyrethroids, with limited technical assistance from PMI. However, in recent years, GoM funding for IRS has also declined. In the 2013 season, only one district was sprayed, and planned spray operations did not occur in 2014 and are unlikely to occur in 2015. GoM spray operations have experienced challenges due to budget reductions and disbursement delays. Without committed funding and technical assistance, it is unlikely that the GoM will be able to effectively support IRS in the future.

Over the past five years, PMI-supported entomological monitoring has documented increasing vector insecticide resistance, including the rise and spread of pyrethroid and carbamate resistance in *An. funestus*, which is the primary malaria vector across most of the country. Pyrethroid resistance in *An. funestus* was first identified in 2010-2011, with permethrin mortality rates of 40 to 92 percent, deltamethrin mortality rates of 41 to 80 percent, and lambdacyhalothrin mortality rates of 32 to 70 percent. According to WHO guidelines, all sampled populations of *An. funestus* were classified as resistant to pyrethroids. Further data from 2014 has shown even higher resistance rates (2 to 14 percent mortality for deltamethrin, 3 to 57 percent for permethrin). Pyrethroid and piperonyl butoxide (PBO) synergist bioassays conducted in Nkhotakota and Chikwawa districts showed a significant increase in mortality, indicating that pyrethroid resistance is partially mediated by mixed-function oxidases (Chikwawa: 14 to 18 percent with pyrethroid alone vs. 80 to 84 percent with PBO; Nkhotakota: 2 to 3 percent with pyrethroid alone vs. 63 percent with PBO).

An. funestus is also resistant to carbamate insecticides. Entomological monitoring data from seven districts collected in 2011 showed that only the population in Mangochi district were fully susceptible to bendiocarb (100 percent mortality). The mortality rate for the Salima population was 96 percent, indicating the possible emergence of resistance, and populations from the remaining districts were resistant according to the WHO guidelines, with less than 90 percent mortality. In 2012, monitoring in seven districts identified resistance to bendiocarb in all sites sampled. Recent 2014 data show mortality rates as low as 4 to 6 percent in Chikwawa and Nkhotakota.

An. arabiensis is the main vector in Karonga District (northern Malawi) and a minor vector in the rest of the country. In 2011, *An. arabiensis* in Karonga were 98-100 percent susceptible to pyrethroids, which the WHO guidelines classify as fully susceptible. However, data from 2014 showed resistance to deltamethrin (58 percent mortality) and permethrin (36 percent); mortality following exposure to bendiocarb was 56 percent. *An. arabiensis* in the rest of the country show similar pyrethroid resistance.

All *An. funestus* populations tested against the organophosphates malathion and pirimiphos-methyl were fully susceptible, while populations tested against DDT were classified as susceptible or suspected resistant. These data indicate organophosphates and possibly DDT are the only technically sound options for IRS in Malawi. However, DDT is currently not registered in Malawi due to environmental concerns and strong opposition from the agricultural sector, which fears that contamination of crops may result in the loss of export markets.

Table 3: IRS activities in Malawi 2013 – 2017[§]

Calendar Year	Number of Districts Sprayed	Insecticide Used	Number of Structures Sprayed	Coverage Rate	Population Protected
2013±	1	Alphacypermethrin	78,965	77%	302,938
2014	3†	Alphacypermethrin	N/A	N/A	N/A
2015*	0	N/A	N/A	N/A	N/A
2016**	3	Organophosphate	TBD	TBD	TBD
2017**	3	Organophosphate	TBD	TBD	TBD

§ PMI has not directly supported IRS operations since 2012.
± Although scheduled for October 2013, IRS activities were implemented in early 2014 due to delays in disbursement of GoM funds. PMI provided technical support through its implementing partner.
† NMCP planned to implement IRS in three districts for the 2014 spray season using GoM funds. At the time of writing, activities have not commenced due to delays in disbursement and it is unclear if IRS will be implemented.
* Represents planning outlined in the draft implementation plan for the Vector Control Strategy 2015-2016. NMCP intends to use this time to prepare for effective spraying in 2016.
** Represents planning outlined in the draft implementation plan for the Vector Control Strategy 2015-2019, which calls for spraying with long-lasting organophosphates in up to three districts. NMCP is working to identify GoM funds for IRS for these spray seasons.

Progress during the last 12-18 months
Given the high levels of pyrethroid resistance observed in *An. funestus* and the recent recommendations of the WHO Global Plan for Insecticide Resistance Management, PMI provided support for the development of an evidence-based IVM strategy for Malawi. The Malaria Vector Control Strategy 2015-2019 was completed in July 2014 but has yet to be signed by senior MOH leadership. The document outlines the Malawi vector control strategy, including ITNs, IRS, larval source management, entomological monitoring and surveillance, and capacity building. The goals for IRS include spraying with non-pyrethroid, non-carbamate insecticides, procurement of WHO Pesticide Evaluation Scheme-recommended insecticides and equipment, and district selection based on epidemiological and entomological data, likely in the high-burden areas primarily along the lakeshore and lower Shire Valley.

The NMCP is currently developing an implementation plan for the Malaria Vector Control Strategy, which is expected to be completed in the coming months. This document will detail specific plans, timelines, budgets, and geographic scope for vector control activities, including IRS.

The NMCP would like to ascertain more detailed information on insecticide resistance throughout Malawi, and has initiated mapping of insecticide resistance with funding from the Global Fund Round 9/Phase 2 grant. Implementation did not start until May 2015 as the amount allocated was significantly lower than needed and the Global Fund disbursement was delayed. The NMCP plans to conduct this surveillance annually in several districts, with the districts sampled rotated from year to year. The PMI team continues to work closely with the NMCP and PMI's entomological surveillance implementing partner to ensure that all monitoring efforts in Malawi are complementary, well-coordinated, and provide the evidence needed for effective programmatic decision-making.

Plans and justification
As part of the draft IVM implementation plan, the GoM has proposed resuming IRS with long-acting organophosphates in three high-burden districts in 2016. Although the future of the IRS program is uncertain due to resource challenges, the GoM has expressed their intent to resume spraying and indicated that they will procure insecticide and fund the operational expenses of the campaign. NMCP has requested technical assistance from PMI to ensure that the campaign is implemented in a timely and effective manner and in compliance with accepted environmental and worker safety standards. Therefore, PMI plans to fund activities to catalyze the IRS campaign, including support for microplanning, geocoding, training, environmental compliance, worker safety, and other logistical activities.

To monitor the implementation of the Vector Control Strategy 2015-2019, PMI will continue to support entomological monitoring in targeted districts. PMI will coordinate with the NMCP on district selection, to complement the NMCP's efforts to map insecticide resistance on a rotating basis and ensure IRS districts are included. Entomological monitoring will include: insecticide resistance monitoring through traditional WHO tube bioassays and newly developed pyrethroid resistance intensity assays; species distribution and abundance; and mosquito behavior, including evaluation of outdoor biting. Currently, PMI Malawi supports resistance testing annually in seven districts. Species abundance is measured monthly in four select districts and quarterly in the remaining three. Given potential upcoming changes to the IRS program, PMI Malawi will work with the NMCP and other stakeholders to determine the appropriate frequency and distribution of future resistance testing and vector density monitoring.

Proposed activities with FY 2016 funding: **($310,000)**
- Technical assistance to NMCP in support of proposed GoM IRS campaign in up to three high-burden districts. Technical assistance to include: microplanning at national and district level (in three districts), geocoding, training of spray operators, worker health and safety, and other logistical activities to support the proposed GoM IRS campaign in up to three high-burden districts ($250,000);

- Environmental compliance support to NMCP for the proposed GoM IRS campaign ($50,000);

- Technical assistance to provide support for development of the IVM implementation plan ($10,000);

- Continued support for entomologic monitoring, with routine surveys of vector density and insecticide resistance testing in one to two sentinel villages in up to seven targeted districts, including any districts where the NMCP conducts IRS (see M&E section).

3. Malaria in pregnancy

NMCP/PMI objectives

The MOH has a three-pronged approach to reducing the burden of malaria in pregnancy: use of IPTp during ANC, distribution of ITNs to pregnant women, and effective case management of malarial illness and anemia. PMI supports all aspects this approach through focused ANC (FANC). The goal of FANC is to provide an integrated package of high impact interventions through four targeted ANC visits. These interventions are intended to ensure that a woman and her fetus survive pregnancy and childbirth in good health. For malaria, IPTp, use of ITNs (for prevention) and effective malaria case management are integrated into FANC. The MOH has updated the national policy on IPTp to reflect the new WHO guidelines. The MOH's objective for IPTp is for at least 80 percent of pregnant women to receive at least three doses of SP during pregnancy. In addition, behavior change messages are communicated at ANC visits and at the community level to maintain and expand demand for IPTp. ITNs are provided to pregnant women at their first ANC visit and again at delivery.

For uncomplicated malaria, the treatment guidelines recommend that during the first trimester quinine plus clindamycin be administered for seven days. In the second and third trimesters of pregnancy, AL is recommended. For the treatment of severe malaria during the first trimester of pregnancy, the treatment guidelines recommend parenteral quinine for at least 24 hours. When the patient is able to take oral medication, quinine and clindamycin are then given to complete the treatment. In the second and third trimesters of pregnancy, parenteral artesunate is recommended for at least 24 hours, followed by AL once the patient is able to take oral medication.

The malaria in pregnancy guidelines recommend the use of iron and folic acid supplementation for the treatment of anemia during pregnancy. Currently, the MOH procures 400 microgram folic acid tablets through the Reproductive Health Directorate's essential drug program.

Progress since PMI was launched

PMI, in conjunction with the NMCP and Reproductive Health Directorate, has worked to increase uptake of IPTp through training and supervision of providers and assistance with directly observed treatment, including supporting infrastructure improvements to assure clean water supply and provision of cups and buckets. Nearly all health workers in the country were trained in the updated IPTp guidance as part of case management trainings in 2014-2015. Through community-based organizations and the small grants program, funds have been made available at the local level to increase demand for ANC and IPTp, encourage women to attend ANC early in their pregnancy in order to receive at least three doses of SP, and promote ITN use among reproductive aged women. PMI has also provided significant support for nationwide BCC efforts to encourage women to adopt these practices.

Nevertheless, despite two decades of IPTp policy in Malawi, coverage goals have yet to be met, even for two doses of IPTp. There are still systemic barriers to seeking ANC in the first trimester, which, in turn, constrain the number of women who can complete the recommended four ANC visits and three or more IPTp doses prior to delivery. Key barriers to ANC attendance include: difficult geographic access to services, particularly in hard-to-reach areas where women may need to travel long distances; lack of supplies and services at facilities; poor attitudes and treatment by health workers, especially toward early care seeking; traditions and cultural norms that discourage revealing a pregnancy in the first trimester; and lack of agency among women, who must wait for consent of their husband or husband's relatives before seeking care.

The percent of women making four or more visits to ANC has dropped steadily from 55 percent in 2000 (DHS 2000) to 44 percent in 2010 (DHS 2010) and remained at 45 percent in 2014 (2014 MICS). Coverage of two doses of IPTp-SP is high in Malawi relative to the rest of sub-Saharan Africa, with 63 percent of pregnant women receiving at least two doses in the 2014 MIS. However, this coverage has not changed substantially over the past five years (60 percent in the 2010 MIS and 54 percent in the 2012 MIS).

Increasing SP resistance represents another significant threat to IPTp in Malawi. In 2012, more than 94 percent of the malaria parasites in pregnant women with asymptomatic parasitemia presenting at an ANC visit at Machinga District Hospital had quintuple mutations for SP resistance, indicating that resistance is almost fixed in this population.[9] A delivery cross-sectional survey at the same hospital found that two or more doses of IPTp with SP during pregnancy compared to zero or one dose was not associated with any reduction in placental malaria for any gravidity.[10] However, two or more doses of IPTp with SP were found to reduce the prevalence of a composite birth outcome among primigravidae (i.e., any of the following: small for gestational age, prematurity, or low birth weight). The conclusion from this study is that two or more doses of IPTp with SP currently provides some small benefit to neonates but does not show the same effect seen in studies conducted when SP was more efficacious in treating *P. falciparum*.

Recent studies from Tanzania and Malawi suggest that the presence of the sextuple mutation in the *P. falciparum* population can result in the failure of SP when given as IPTp. Currently, the presence of the sextuple mutant in Malawi is less than 10 percent, however, this prevalence is expected to continue to rise. In addition to monitoring the prevalence of SP resistance markers using samples collected from the 2014 therapeutic efficacy study (TES), PMI plans to support a study assessing the efficacy of a newer antimalarial, dihydroartemisinin-piperaquine, as a replacement for SP to be given as IPTp using FY 2013 funds.

Awareness campaigns and provision of ITNs through ANC clinics support the use of ITNs during pregnancy. In the 2014 MIS, 62 percent of pregnant women reported sleeping under an ITN the night before, however, this figure jumps to 85 percent when considering only pregnant women in household with at least one ITN. As access seems to be a significant factor in the overall utilization, use of ITNs among pregnant women is expected to improve following the mass distribution campaign in 2015. Efforts to improve accountability for case management

---

[9] Mwandama D, personal communication, 2012
[10] Gutman J. et al., 2013.

commodities will also include efforts to improve practices for routine distribution of ITNs at ANC (see pharmaceutical management section).

Progress during the last 12-18 months
With support from PMI, the MOH updated the national policy on IPTp to reflect the new WHO guidelines. The revised policy removes previous barriers to IPTp uptake, under which women were only to receive IPTp at specific intervals during pregnancy. This expanded guidance should improve the uptake of IPTp by allowing women visiting ANC later in their pregnancy to take three or more doses of SP (see Malaria in Pregnancy: *NMCP/PMI Objectives*). Nearly all health workers were trained in these new guidelines during the case management trainings in 2014-15.

PMI continued to support routine distribution of ITNs through ANC (please see ITN section). PMI also continued to support appropriate case management of malaria in pregnant women through the procurement of antimalarial drugs, outreach training, supportive supervision in health facilities, and behavior change communication for prompt care seeking through the integrated communication platform.

Commodity gap analysis

Table 4. SP Gap Analysis

Calendar Year	2015	2016	2017
Total Population	16,310,430	16,832,908	17,371,561
SP Needs			
Total number of potential pregnant women attending ANC*	815,522	841,645	868,578
Total number of ANC visits for IPTp	1,549,491	1,767,455	1,954,301
Total SP Need (in treatments)*	**1,549,491$^{\pm}$**	**1,767,455†**	**1,954,301**
Partner Contributions			
SP carried over (deficit) from previous year	4,600,513	3,051,022	0$^{\infty}$
SP from MOH	0	0	0
SP from Global Fund	0	0	0
SP from Other Donors	0	0	0
SP planned with PMI funding	0	0	2,000,000
Total SP Available	**4,600,513**	**3,051,022**	**2,000,000**
Total SP Surplus (Gap)	**3,051,022**	**1,283,567**	**45,699**

* The total number of pregnant women is estimated as 5% of the total population.
± Assumes 95% of pregnant women receive the first dose of IPTp, 70% receive the second, and 25% receive the third.
† Assumes 95% of pregnant women will receive the first dose of IPTp, 75% receive the second, and 40% receive the third.
§Assumes 95% will receive the first dose, 80% will receive the second, and 50% receive the third. Estimates of need will be reevaluated in 2016.
∞ Most currently available SP will expire at the end of 2016 and cannot be carried over to 2017.

Plans and justification

Despite high first attendance at ANC clinics (90 percent), IPTp goals in Malawi have not yet been met. Although the integration of IPTp into focused ANC services helps assure that SP for IPTp is available in all health centers and administered by trained personnel, since IPTp is one among many services offered at ANC there could be dilution of impact. PMI will continue to support supervision and mentoring of ANC providers on the revised IPTp guidelines.

With FY 2016 funding, PMI will continue integrated and malaria-specific behavior change communication activities in support of IPTp, case management, and ITN use at national and community levels (see BCC section). In addition, PMI will continue to provide free ITNs for routine distribution at ANC visits and at labor and delivery for newborns (see ITN section). PMI will procure SP and supplies to ensure directly observed therapy and improved IPTp uptake at ANC. PMI will continue funding to support supervision activities for malaria in pregnancy interventions as part of the focused antenatal care package. Furthermore, through its support to strengthen the HMIS system, PMI will help improve the collection of data on IPTp.

Proposed activities with FY 2016 funding: **($750,000)**
- Continue to support routine distribution of ITNs through ANC and maternity clinics (see ITN section);
- Procurement of SP for IPTp (2 million treatments) ($300,000);
- Procurement of ANC supplies (cups and water buckets) to help improve IPTp uptake through directly observed treatment ($50,000);
- Continued support for strengthening focused antenatal care in 10 PMI focus districts through production of SOPs, training, supervision visits, and mentoring health providers ($400,000);
- Continue to support BCC for malaria in pregnancy interventions: early case management, IPTp, and ITNs (see BCC section); and
- Continue to support central level routine HMIS to collect routine data on MIP (see M&E section).

4. Case management

a. Diagnosis and Treatment

NMCP/PMI objectives
Increasing capacity to ensure prompt and effective case management and reduce the presumptive use of antimalarial medications is a key priority in Malawi's Malaria Strategic Plan. To achieve this increased capacity, the MOH is focusing its efforts in the following areas:
1) Ensuring consistent availability of high-quality diagnostic and treatment commodities through proper quantification, procurement, and distribution
2) Strengthening quality assurance for malaria diagnostics
3) Training and supervising health workers on malaria case management at all levels of the health system
4) Supporting and expanding community case management in hard-to-reach areas (i.e., community level)

In the *Guidelines for the Treatment of Malaria in Malawi*, the MOH recommends testing all suspected malaria cases using an RDT prior to initiating treatment. Microscopy is recommended for the following purposes: 1) to confirm malaria diagnosis in hospitalized patients with suspected severe malaria; 2) to monitor treatment progress in severe malaria cases receiving parenteral treatment; and 3) to confirm first-line treatment failures. The *Guidelines for the Treatment of Malaria in Malawi* recommends AL as the first-line treatment and artesunate-amodiaquine (ASAQ) as the second-line treatment. Oral quinine plus clindamycin is recommended for the treatment of uncomplicated malaria in pregnant women in the first trimester and for children weighing less than five kilograms. For the management of patients with severe malaria, parenteral artesunate is recommended as the definitive treatment and as pre-referral treatment in health centers. A draft policy covering the use of RDTs and rectal artesunate by HSAs at the community level is currently under review and is expected to be approved in the near future.

Progress since PMI was launched
Since Malawi became a PMI focus country in 2007, PMI has supported the procurement of malaria commodities including RDTs and malaria medicines. To date, PMI has procured 16.1 million RDTs, 32.5 million ACT treatments, 550,000 vials of injectable artesunate, and 50,000 artesunate suppositories.

In 2007, Malawi changed the first-line medication for uncomplicated malaria from SP to AL, with ASAQ as the second-line treatment. PMI has supported the training and supervision of health workers on the appropriate management of malaria and the promotion of appropriate care seeking and treatment adherence behaviors through national-level mass media and community mobilization channels.

Before 2010, Malawi's national malaria policy recommended diagnostic testing prior to treatment only for individuals over five years of age. Guidelines recommended presumptive treatment for children less than five years of age, due in part to the high prevalence of malaria and limited diagnostic capacity in-country.

In 2010, the GoM updated its policy to include the use of RDTs for malaria diagnosis for all suspected cases. To help ensure an effective transition from largely presumptive treatment to universal diagnostic testing, the MOH adopted a phased approach for the roll-out of malaria RDTs. Phase one, which began in July 2011 and is now complete, focused on the distribution and use of malaria RDTs at health facilities. PMI supported this phase of the roll-out, including technical assistance for guideline development, commodity procurement and distribution, and healthcare worker training. Following a successful feasibility study of the use of RDTs by HSAs, the national policy was updated to officially allow HSAs to use RDTs. This will allow phase two of the RDT roll-out, which extends the use of RDTs to the community level, to start in 2015.

To strengthen diagnostic capacity, in 2010, PMI supported the introduction of a quality assurance program designed to improve Malawi's clinical and laboratory diagnostic services. This program as focused on the provision of outreach training and supportive supervision (OTSS) to laboratory and clinical supervisors. The OTSS intervention provides on-site training and long-term, ongoing support to strengthen diagnostic and treatment services in health facilities. During scheduled visits, supervisors identify areas for improvement and provide immediate feedback to laboratory and clinical staff. Currently, OTSS occurs at all health facilities in Malawi. In general, facilities receive four quarterly visits at enrollment and then two per year after minimum compliance standards are met.

In 2013, the MOH revised the *Guidelines for the Treatment of Malaria in Malawi* to replace quinine with parenteral artesunate for the pre-referral and definitive treatment of severe malaria at the health facility level and introduce rectal artesunate for pre-referral treatment of severe malaria at the community level. PMI provided technical guidance and funding for this policy change and the drafting and printing of the revised guidelines and associated training manuals.

Progress during the last 12-18 months
PMI has worked closely with the NMCP and the Global Fund to coordinate procurement and delivery schedules to ensure that appropriate central stock levels of antimalarials and RDTs were maintained. For the past year, PMI procured approximately 4.8 million RDTs and 5.2 million ACTs. The past year also saw the near completion of training of over 8,000 facility-based healthcare workers. To date, the rollout of parenteral artesunate has been completed nationwide and roll-out of rectal artesunate is ongoing.

Results from a 2011 antimalarial TES were released in early 2015 and showed a 93.4 percent PCR-corrected cure rate using AL.[11] A TES conducted in 2014 shows continued high efficacy of both AL and ASAQ, with PCR corrected cure rates for both drugs greater than 99 percent (see the *Plans and justification* section for discussion of future TES). An EUV study conducted in early 2015 showed that 88 percent of children under five years with malaria were treated with AL. The same evaluation revealed stockouts of all AL formulations occurring in 2 percent of facilities and an understock rate of 43.9 percent.

PMI continued to support the strengthening of diagnostic services through the OTSS program. During this past year, PMI supported the eleventh round of OTSS, including visits to 242 health facilities in 29 districts, the supervision and training of nearly 1,000 health workers, and the training of 37 laboratory supervisors (out of a total of 40) in advanced malaria diagnostic training. These endeavors, in combination with previous efforts, have focused on negative test adherence, RDT use (preparation and interpretation) in health facilities, and microscopy (preparation, staining, and reading).

Currently, approximately 30 percent of health facilities have the capacity to provide malaria microscopy by trained and qualified laboratory staff. Expansion of microscopy services to additional facilities is limited by the lack of trained health workers, inconsistent electrical supply, and inadequate laboratory equipment and supplies. Even within facilities with trained and qualified staff, power supply interruptions and supply stockouts constrain microscope use.

The recent roll-out of RDTs to all health facilities has expanded diagnostic capacity, particularly for facilities lacking the capacity to perform malaria microscopy. Overall, this has reduced the reliance on presumptive diagnosis and moved Malawi closer to universal diagnostic coverage. Through its implementing partner, PMI is supporting the development of a national slide archive to assist with quality assurance of microscopy. Challenges to reaching the goal of universal

---

[11] Dambe R, Sande J, Ali D, et al. Monitoring the efficacy of artemether-lumefantrine for the treatment of uncomplicated malaria in Malawian children. *Malaria Journal* 2015;14:175.

diagnostic coverage include inadequate diagnostic technical capacity (including human resources), shortages of diagnostic supplies at health facilities, and the current lack of training of HSAs in the use of RDTs.

ACT consumption has outpaced reported malaria cases, with approximately 10.5 million ACTs consumed compared to approximately 6 million malaria cases (per HMIS data) in 2014 necessitating an emergency shipment of 3 million ACTs earlier this year in order to prevent a nationwide shortage. Multiple sessions with the NMCP, Global Fund, and implementing partners were convened to identify potential reasons for this discrepancy and to develop approaches to rectifying it. Preliminary investigations have identified the facility level—as opposed to central or district—as the most problematic. The consensus is that the problem is multifactorial, with continued presumptive treatment, poor record keeping, and theft as the likely main contributors. A lack of legal enforcement (e.g., minimal fines for those caught with stolen medications) creates an enabling environment for continued theft. Other contributing factors include stock mismanagement, inadequate facilities for commodity storage, and patients often receiving a diagnosis and treatment at different locations within the facility, which leads to additional record keeping challenges. An action plan has been created with the input from the NMCP and is discussed in the Pharmaceutical Management section.

Malawi implements integrated community case management, with national guidance emphasizing implementation in areas more than five kilometers from a healthcare facility. Approximately 3,190 village health clinics exist nationwide and PMI currently provides support to nearly all of the 1,738 village health clinics located in the 15 districts targeted by PMI's integrated service delivery partner. Activities include equipping village health clinics and providing training, printing registers, and supervision/monitoring of HSAs. HSAs, who are paid health workers, have been trained on the administration of ACTs and are currently providing presumptive treatment of malaria at the community level. A study of RDT use by HSAs was recently completed and verified the feasibility and acceptability of this modality. After initial delays, rollout of RDTs to the community level is expected to commence in 2015. In addition, PMI supported community mobilization activities in the 15 targeted districts to increase malaria prevention and care-seeking behaviors by community members.

Commodity gap analysis

Table 5: RDT Gap Analysis

Calendar Year	2015	2016	2017
RDT Needs			
Target population at risk for malaria	16,310,430	16,832,908	17,371,561
Total RDT Needs*	**11,132,839**	**13,030,849**	**12,311,814**
Partner Contributions			
RDTs carried over from previous year	2,300,580	614,518	0
RDTs from MOH	0	4,429,852	4,105,404
RDTs from Global Fund	646,777	4,429,850	4,105,404
RDTs from Other Donors	0	0	
RDTs planned with PMI funding	8,800,000$^{\pm}$	2,900,000	4,100,000
Total RDTs Available	**11,747,357**	**12,374,220**	**12,310,808**
Total RDT Surplus (Gap) [†]	**614,518**	**(656,629)** [§]	**(1,006)**

* The total RDT need is based on the 2015 National Quantification of Health Commodities (publication forthcoming), which utilizes past consumption and the Roll Back Malaria Gap Analysis tool as the basis for projecting need. At this time, the national health information system does not have reliable data on fever cases from which to extrapolate RDT needs.

$\pm$ Includes 4 million RDTs approved in the FY 13 MOP, 3.3 million RDTs approved in the FY 14 MOP, and 1.5 million RDTs procured in early 2015 using savings from past commodity procurements.

† Estimated gap does not include required buffer stock of RDTs to maintain sufficient quantities in the pipeline.

§ Given recent reductions in RDT prices, PMI expects to be able to procure additional RDTs with FY15 funding to cover this gap.

Table 6: ACT Gap Analysis

Calendar Year	2015	2016	2017
ACT Needs			
Target population at risk for malaria	16,310,430	16,832,908	17,371,561
Total ACT Needs[*]	**10,521,224**	**9,476,813**	**8,907,693**
Partner Contributions			
ACTs carried over from previous year	3,000,000	1,878,776	
ACTs from MOH			2,295,551
ACTs from Global Fund	2,000,000	5,943,271	1,731,732
ACTs from Other Donors			
ACTs planned with PMI funding	7,400,000[±]	0	3,500,000
Total ACTs Available	**12,400,000**	**7,822,047**	**7,527,283**
Total ACT Surplus (Gap) †	**1,878,776**	**(1,654,766)**[§]	**(1,380,410)**

* The total ACT needs are based on the 2015 National Quantification of Health Commodities (publication forthcoming), which utilizes past consumption and the Roll Back Malaria Gap Analysis tool as the basis for projecting need. The national health management information system does not currently have reliable malaria case data, so past consumption has been used as a proxy for malaria cases.
± Includes 2,200,000 from FY 2014 received in 2015, 3,000,000 procured in early 2015 using savings from past commodity procurements, and 2,200,000 from FY 2015 that are projected to arrive and be distributed in 2015.
† Estimated gap does not include required buffer stock of ACTs to maintain sufficient quantities in the pipeline.
§ Efforts to improve accountability and reporting around malaria cases and commodities are commencing in July 2015. It is hoped that these efforts will result in reduced ACT consumption and reduce the gap expected in 2016 and 2017.

Planned RDTs are expected to be sufficient to meet the estimated need in Malawi through 2017, but stock levels will require continuous monitoring as RDTs are extended to the community level. However, at the time of writing, stockouts of ACTs are expected in 2016 and 2017, even if all planned procurements arrive in a timely manner. As described above and in the pharmaceutical management section, PMI and other partners are working closely with MOH to address high consumption of ACTs and improve overall accountability for commodities. Although this may reduce improve the situation in the medium to longer term, PMI is concerned about the current consumption of ACTs and continues to highlight this issue with key stakeholders.

PMI remains committed to supporting MOH efforts to provide prompt, appropriate, and effective malaria treatment. With FY 2016 funding, PMI will focus on improving community and facility-based case management services in ten priority districts, those with the highest malaria burden in the country. Case management commodities, specifically RDTs and ACTs, will still be supplied nationwide. Parenteral and rectal artesunate for severe malaria treatment will not be procured with PMI funds because of a projected surplus in the country and the availability of other donor support for these commodities (e.g., Global Fund, Medicines for Malaria Venture).

In order to expand diagnostic and treatment capabilities in the community, PMI will support training of HSAs in the use of RDTs and pre-referral use of rectal artesunate. Although nearly all facility-based healthcare workers have received initial training in case management, follow-up supervisory visits will assess effectiveness of these trainings and identify areas needing further attention with supervision. PMI will continue to support and expand a core group of microscopy trainers to improve the quality of microscopy services. In order to further enhance microscopy capabilities, a national archive of malaria slides is being created with PMI support, with initial efforts focusing on procurement of equipment for training and later efforts focusing on donor collection and validation.

The Global Fund will support a TES in calendar year 2016. PMI will not fund or implement this study, but will still offer to perform k13 artemisinin resistance testing. PMI funding will also target BCC interventions focused on appropriate care seeking behavior and medication adherence for both uncomplicated and severe malaria at the community level (see BCC section).

Proposed activities with FY 2016 funding: (**$8,012,000**)

- Procure 4.1 million RDTs (distribution costs covered in Pharmaceutical Management section) ($1,517,000);
- Procure 3.5 million AL treatment courses (distribution costs covered in Pharmaceutical Management section) ($4,270,000);
- Procure ancillary diagnostic supplies (gloves and sharps containers) for RDT implementation ($150,000);
- Case management support in ten focus districts, concentrating on RDT use and adherence to results, appropriate use of severe malaria treatments, and supervision and mentorship in facility and community settings, with approximately 80 percent effort to facility settings and 20 percent effort to the community level ($1,325,000); and
- Case management support in ten focus districts, concentrating on quality improvement/quality control for diagnostics in facility and community settings ($750,000).

b. Pharmaceutical Management

NMCP/PMI objectives

The 2011-2016 Malaria Strategic Plan calls for a reliable, secure, and accountable pharmaceutical and supply chain management system to ensure the consistent availability of essential commodities and supplies for malaria control and prevention activities. To achieve this objective, the NMCP plans to conduct annual forecasting and quantification, strengthen the logistics management information systems in collaboration with Health Technical Support Services (HTSS), develop annual procurement plans in collaboration with partners, and support national and international efforts to strengthen the procurement and supply chain system.

Progress since PMI was launched

Supply chain issues have been a key concern in Malawi. Due to issues of leakage and general mismanagement, a PMI-Global Fund supply chain was created in late 2010 to distribute all USG and Global Fund supported malaria commodities. In mid-2011, CMST reached the point of near-collapse when its procurement systems became de-capitalized due to continued non-payment of arrears by district governments. In response, the GoM submitted an emergency request for procurement support from health donors, which resulted in the creation of an 18-month multi-donor emergency essential drugs project.

In August 2012, representatives from the GoM, CMST, and several partners, including WHO, the Global Fund, DFID, and PMI, conducted a review of the supply chain management system and developed a _Joint Strategy for Supply Chain Integration in Malawi_. The roadmap included four distinct phases of integration, including CMST recapitalization and reform, management of essential drugs supply chain, warehousing and distribution, and procurement functions. Thirty-six specific performance benchmarks will be measured through ad hoc external assessments and a mid-term review of CMST's capabilities as pre-conditions for re-integration.

In addition to support for CMS reform, the USG has supported efforts to improve the overall supply chain through continued support to the MOH to strengthen planning and coordination centrally and improve commodity management and reporting at the district and facility levels. Support to the central level has included technical assistance to implement annual national quantification and forecasting of all essential medicines, conduct supply planning and commodity monitoring, maintain Supply Chain Manager and the National Stock Status Database, and provide financial support to employ two technical assistants seconded to HTSS, which has supervisory authority over the CMS. Support to the district, health center, and community levels have included quarterly supervision, mentoring, and EUV surveys; expanded access to Supply Chain Manager for LMIS; and improved access to malaria commodities through iCCM.

Progress during the last 12-18 months

The NMCP and PMI continued to focus on minimizing or eliminating stockouts of malaria commodities at service delivery points and strengthening supply planning and commodity management through planning, training, and supportive supervision. PMI-supported activities conducted in 2014 included monthly commodity distributions, integrated supportive supervision and peer mentoring, LMIS reporting, two EUVs, and capacity building at the central, district, and facility levels. After dedicated efforts by PMI and MOH to improve LMIS reporting, rates have remained high, at over 80 percent.

PMI plans to continue using a parallel supply chain that distributes USAID-procured health commodities. However, costs to operate it are expected to increase and coordination of malaria commodity distribution will be more challenging due to fragmentation of parallel supply chains in the past year. After utilizing the PMI supply chain implementing partner for several years, the Global Fund began a new warehousing and distribution contract for Global Fund-procured malaria commodities late in 2014. While this resulted in a consolidated parallel supply chain for all Global Fund-procured commodities (i.e., HIV, TB, and malaria), there are now multiple parallel supply chains for malaria. Additionally, artesunate procured by Medicines for Malaria Venture/UNITAID is now distributed by CMST, creating a third malaria supply chain.

There has been some limited progress recently on a roadmap for supply chain integration. A committee has been established to oversee implementation of the *Joint Strategy for Supply Chain Integration* that was agreed to by GoM and development partners in 2012. However, only two meetings have been held, in January and June 2015. Plans are underway to conduct an independent evaluation of CMST's progress toward the agreed-upon benchmarks and to assess the potential for absorbing donor-funded commodities. Though these long overdue developments are positive, it is not clear when PMI will be able to transition the warehousing and distribution of malaria commodities to CMST. PMI, through the USAID Mission, will continue to advocate strongly for rapid and effective strengthening of the national supply chain system and will reevaluate a reintegration timeline after the independent evaluation of CMST progress and capacity is complete.

Consumption trends for ACTs have continued to increase over the past two years, from roughly 9 million ACTs in 2013, to 10.5 million ACTs in 2014. In the same period, reported malaria cases have also increased, but the very substantial gap between AL consumption and reported cases has continued to widen; in 2014 only 6 million cases were reported through the national HMIS, including 1.2 million presumed cases from iCCM. Given this large discrepancy, PMI supported a rapid assessment of case reporting and ACT consumption in 47 facilities in November 2014. The assessment report is still pending, but results indicate several drivers for the high and increasing consumption, including poor case reporting through the HMIS, lack of provider compliance with RDT results, widespread use of ACTs without confirmation at the community level, and theft of commodities at the facility and perhaps community level. Working with NMCP and other partners, PMI has developed an action plan to improve commodity oversight and management – including improved supervision at the district, facility and community levels, better use of data for decision making, and audits of facilities with discrepancies between consumption and reported cases. Based on reconciliation of cases with commodities used, it is likely that malaria case data will play a greater role in commodity planning in the coming year. Additionally, the recent training of health workers in malaria case management included an emphasis on compliance with RDTs and appropriate use of ACTs, which, when coupled with appropriate follow up and supervision, should improve provider behavior.

Plans and justification

Given the uncertain timelines for reintegration with CMST, PMI remains committed to supporting the operation of the PMI-USAID supply chain. In support of this, PMI will strengthen MOH commodity management and planning at all levels of the system. PMI and the USG will continue to monitor and support the ongoing CMST reform and transition to determine when to reenter the CMST system. At the district, facility, and community levels, PMI will continue to focus on improving provider behavior, accountability for medicines, and improved data management.

Proposed activities with FY 2016 funding: **($2,500,000)**

- Provide technical assistance to GoM to improve management, oversight, and accountability for supply chain and logistics management. Activities include: building leadership and human capacity for supply chain management, strengthening district supply chains, supporting efforts to transition to an updated electronic LMIS, enabling appropriate oversight and quality assurance, improving pharmaceutical management at facilities, and ensuring strong coordination between key stakeholders ($1,000,000); and
- Provide support for receipt, warehousing, management and oversight, and physical distribution of PMI-procured case management commodities through the PMI supply chain management system directly to the health facility level ($1,500,000).

5. Health system strengthening and capacity building

PMI supports a broad array of health system strengthening activities which cut across intervention areas, such as training of health workers, supply chain management and health information systems strengthening, drug quality monitoring, and NMCP capacity building.

NMCP/PMI objectives

The Malaria Strategic Plan 2011-2016 calls for strengthening capacity in program management at all levels of health service delivery by providing policy direction and leadership, building human resource capacity, mobilizing and utilizing resources more effectively, improving coordination, and strengthening procurement and supply chain management. The NMCP plans to achieve these goals through strong leadership; creation of a supportive environment; improved infrastructure, equipment and supplies; and effective collaboration with partners.

Progress since PMI was launched

The USG has taken an integrated approach to contribute to efficient systems strengthening across the Malawian health sector. To that end, the USG has helped to train and retain health care workers; incentivized health workers to deliver higher quality services; built the capacity of the MOH to effectively utilize the LMIS and improve coordination of donor drug procurement; expanded health information systems and linked these systems across health programs; and provided broad-based support to the national laboratory system. The USG also has supported the development of leadership and management systems at the MOH and district levels, including systems for human resources, monitoring and evaluation, and finance management.

USAID has leveraged and created synergies with many other partners, including the private sector. The USG agencies have served as chairs on the Education, Agriculture, and Nutrition Donor Groups in addition to the Health Donor Group. Furthermore, USAID is a member of the Malawi Country Coordinating Mechanism for the Global Fund grants and the USAID Health Director is a member of the CMST supply chain integration oversight task force.

The Malawi 2011-2016 National HSSP builds upon the sustained gains made under the 2004-2010 Program of Work, and places an emphasis on primary health care. Considerable improvements in the delivery of an EHP have been reflected by reduced infant and child mortality rates, pneumonia case fatality and maternal mortality, and in maintaining high immunization coverage, among other areas. However, while overall curative services are improving, services are not yet spread equitably across the country and health promotion and prevention activities lag behind. Utilization of ANC and postnatal care is not increasing as planned, and quality and availability of essential obstetric care is limited by shortages of skilled human resources, equipment, and transport. In the absence of donor funding, the resources for general health services are minimal and the technical capacities of personnel are limited (see Part 10: Challenges and Opportunities in the Strategy section). Health centers and hospitals continue to struggle with shortages of medicines and supplies.

In the area of monitoring and evaluation, while systems have been developed, data quality and analysis remain weak, prompting several disease control programs to implement parallel surveillance systems. In principle, available systems are capable of producing reliable and timely data, but the limited capacity at the facility and district level hinder successful implementation. The M&E system in MOH is not robust enough to handle the multitude of indicators in various programs and CMED does not yet have the capacity to perform thorough analysis of progress in the health sector.

Progress during the last 12-18 months

Through its implementing partners, PMI provides technical support to the MOH to help improve policies, management and leadership, and fiscal responsibility. PMI promotes evidence-based policies, strengthens the management and technical capacity of the NMCP and other MOH divisions, supports development and strengthening of electronic data systems, strengthens the zonal supervision structures, bolsters decentralized management of health services at the district level, and strengthens the government's capacity for financial planning and management and budget execution. Key activities during the past year include:

- *Policy*: PMI is strengthening the policy development unit within the MOH and has initiated support for the revision of the National Malaria Policy.
- *Human resources development*: USG has supported training and coaching of 65 key staff members of the MOH on leadership and management at the Malawi Institute of Management. PMI strengthens NMCP's capacity to better manage Global Fund grants by providing direct technical support for grant writing and negotiations, financial management coaching, and ongoing support to NMCP's M&E efforts. PMI also began supporting the two-year pre-service training program for pharmacy assistants in 2015.
- *Electronic data systems*: PMI provided ongoing support to the DHIS 2 platform. In addition, an electronic data tool (using tablets and mobile phones) for integrated supportive supervision was finalized and is being used in 15 targeted districts as well as by zonal and national management teams. The tool includes malaria indicators for IPTp, ITNs, and adherence to case management guidelines.

PMI built human resource capacity through the training of health facility workers on malaria case management and prevention of malaria in pregnancy, laboratory technicians on diagnosis of malaria, and pharmacists and other relevant health workers on pharmaceutical management. In addition, PMI strengthens supply chain management systems by providing technical assistance to HTSS in the MOH as well as to the district and facilities levels (see case management section). Furthermore, PMI works with other USG health programs to improve health information systems through technical assistance and capacity building (see M&E section).

Working closely with other USG programs in Malawi, PMI will support the implementation of the HSSP. Although PMI continues to address malaria-specific challenges, nationwide progress will require increased attention to strengthening the overall health system with in-country partners. PMI Malawi plans to focus and concentrate its service delivery strengthening efforts in ten high malaria burden districts, building government capacity for facility-based case management, FANC and delivery of IPTp, community mobilization and iCCM, and monitoring and evaluation at the district level. These capacity building efforts will include training and expanded supportive supervision and mentoring to relevant cadres (e.g., facility and community health care workers, pharmacy technicians and assistants, etc.). Simultaneously, at the central level, PMI will provide technical and operational support to the NMCP and other key parts of the MOH (such as CMED and IMCI), support policy development and dissemination, strengthen pharmaceutical supply chain management, and reinforce the HMIS and monitoring and evaluation.

Proposed activities with FY 2016 funding: **($1,360,000)**

- Support to malaria district coordinators, district health officers, and zonal health officers: PMI will support key district health staff to conduct facility and community-level supportive supervision, mentorship, coaching, and assistance with data collection and reporting, as well as support to the zonal offices for improved supervision and oversight ($300,000);
- Support to NMCP to hold technical working group and research dissemination meetings and support basic operational functioning (e.g. printing, IT and other equipment maintenance, internet time). This is a continuation of an activity started with FY 2013 funding ($240,000);
- Support NMCP to participate in short courses and regional and international meetings to expand knowledge base and increase NMCP capacity to implement an evidence-based malaria program in line with international guidelines and standards ($30,000);
- Build capacity and central-level support for MOH Central Monitoring and Evaluation Division (CMED) ($200,000);
- Improve facility-level commodity storage capacity: PMI plans to complement other USG investments to improve storage conditions at select facilities with high malaria burden by providing support for a limited number of pre-fabricated storage containers for health facilities ($300,000);
- Pre-service training of pharmacy assistants: PMI plans to continue to provide scholarships for 48 pharmacy assistants (24 students per cohort in a 2-year pre-service pharmacy assistant training), so that this cadre will enter the workforce with the stock management skills necessary to help ensure commodity security at the facility level ($200,000);
- Revision of pre-service curricula: Currently, curricula for health care providers (e.g., medical assistants and nurses), pharmacists, and lab technicians do not reflect the most up-to-date technical guidelines. Improving the quality of pre-service training is expected to reduce the necessity for in-service training. Thus, PMI will support updating pre-

service curricula at training institutions to ensure health workers entering the workforce have received training on the current malaria guidelines and practices ($50,000);

- Provide support to Peace Corps: $10,000 for small project assistance grants and $30,000 to support three malaria coordinators ($40,000); and
- Provide ongoing support for an operational research and best practices dissemination forum: Using FY 2014 and FY 2015 funds, PMI plans to continue to provide ongoing support for an operational research and best practices dissemination forum. This forum routinely shares research findings and provides status updates of ongoing research activities in order to foster better coordination between academia, research institutions, and the NMCP and to help ensure that findings from operational research inform policy development and programmatic decisions ($0 – supported with previous years funds).

Table 7: Health Systems Strengthening Activities

HSS Building Block	Technical Area	Description of Activity
Health Services	MIP	Strengthening FANC and improving IPTp uptake
	Diagnosis and treatment	Strengthening case management at facility and community levels
	Diagnosis and treatment	Supporting quality of diagnosis at facility and community levels
Health Workforce	HSS	Pre-service training of pharmacy assistants
	HSS	Support to district malaria coordinators, district health offices, and zonal health offices
	HSS	Building capacity of MOH Central Monitoring and Evaluation Division
	M&E	Strengthen routine HMIS at the district and central levels
Essential Medical Products, Vaccines, and Technologies	ITNs	Procurement and distribution of ITNs
	IRS	Technical assistance to NMCP to support IRS, environmental compliance, and IVM implementation
	Diagnosis and treatment	Procurement and distribution of RDTs, ACTs, ancillary supplies
	Pharmaceutical Management	Supply chain strengthening
Health Finance	n/a	n/a
Leadership and Governance	HSS	Support to NMCP for professional development and conferences
	Pharmaceutical management	Technical assistance to GoM to improve management, oversight, and accountability for supply chain and logistics management

6. Behavior change communication

NMCP/PMI objectives

The HSSP 2011–2016 emphasizes the need to recognize and scale up health promotion interventions in the implementation of the EHP. The HSSP 2011–2016 identified the limited capacity of existing communication efforts to reach all segments of the population as a threat to the successful delivery of essential health packages through public health interventions. In line with the HSSP, the 2011-2016 National Malaria Strategic Plan calls for strengthening advocacy, communication, and social mobilization capacities to move towards optimal coverage for all malaria interventions. This is aimed at achieving above 80 percent of the population practicing positive behavior to prevention and control of malaria by 2016. The 2011-2016 National Malaria Strategic Plan aims to educate communities to practice appropriate preventive behaviors and to seek prompt diagnosis and treatment of malaria at the onset of signs and symptoms.

To achieve this, the NMCP has put in place the Malaria Communication Strategy (2011–2015) whose goal is to improve behavioral change interventions through advocacy and social mobilization. (The Malawi Health Communication Strategy 2015–2020 is in the approval process.) Advocacy is targeted at the national level to mobilize political commitment and resources for malaria prevention and control efforts, stimulate increased responsibility on the part of community members to adopt malaria control behaviors, and encourage clinicians to adhere to case management and malaria in pregnancy guidelines. This strategy uses the *Life is Precious, Take care of it (Moyo ndi Mpamba, Usamalireni)* slogan, which is popular among Malawians and has been adopted as the central vehicle for health promotion activities for all 13 EHPs. It provides a harmonious platform that all program areas can leverage to effectively reach Malawians with comprehensive health information. This strategy is designed to be implemented through District Health Promotion Officers, Health Surveillance Assistants, Village Health Committees, and Village Development Committees.

The NMCP established a technical committee to support and guide the implementation of the Malaria Communication Strategy. This committee is comprised of key malaria and BCC stakeholders, including PMI. During major events and massive interventions such as universal ITN campaigns, task forces under this committee spearhead BCC efforts to support the intervention (e.g., logistics, resource mobilization, community engagement, technical direction).

Progress since PMI was launched
PMI Malawi supports an integrated approach to BCC focused on ITNs, MIP, and case management. BCC activities have included: national campaigns and door-to-door visits to promote year-round ITN use; large-scale campaigns to emphasize ANC attendance to improve IPTp uptake; and community-based campaigns that emphasize ITN utilization, as well as improved case management through the promotion of early care-seeking behavior.

Results from the MIS 2014 suggest that BCC efforts have been effective in conveying information that led to adoption of positive behavior. Approximately 84 percent of Malawian women reported having knowledge that sleeping under a mosquito net can prevent malaria infections. In terms of behavioral practices, for instance, in households that own at least one ITN, ITN utilization among children under the age of five years and pregnant women was 1.2 times higher in 2014 than in 2012. Similarly, household ownership of ITNs increased to 70 percent in 2014 from 55 percent in 2012. Although the causal link and quantification of contribution is difficult to establish, it would be reasonable to assume that BCC efforts contributed to improved ITN use in households in Malawi.

BCC strategies have been employed from the national to the community level to target policy makers, health care providers, and community members. In promoting malaria interventions, PMI has utilized a variety of BCC approaches, including educational meetings, mass media, print media, community drama, and interpersonal communication activities. At the national level, PMI has been implementing BCC activities through an integrated social BCC mechanism. The objectives of this project are in line with the NMCP's strategic plan to build capacity of key national institutional partners, strengthen national and community level planning and coordination, develop and produce evidence-based BCC packages under a multi-level media campaign, and identify and implement best practices.

The small grants program for community mobilization has remained a central component of the BCC strategy to ensure good coverage and reach of BCC activities at household level in all districts where PMI's implementing partners work. Under this program, teams consisting of HSAs and community health extension workers collaborate with the communities to identify key health issues. The teams then helps the community identify solutions to these issues in an effort to bring about appropriate behavior for improved health outcomes. At the household and village level, communications teams have also concentrated on interpersonal communication activities to promote prevention behaviors including early and frequent ANC attendance, appropriate and prompt health-seeking behaviors and ITN use.

Progress during the last 12-18 months
PMI-funded activities helped strengthen national-level and targeted district-level BCC planning and coordination on EHP priorities. Specific activities included: support for inclusion of BCC in health sector district implementation plans, health promotion and communication technical working group meetings, and the development of a National Health Promotion Policy.

PMI funding supported strengthening BCC planning and coordination at national and district levels through the development of the National Malawi Health Communication Strategy (2015 – 2020), which is designed coordinate health promotion and communication strategies across the Health Sector, and the National Malaria Communication Strategy (2015 –2020), which harmonizes communication approaches to encourage adoption of positive health behaviors.

PMI funding also supported the MOH's efforts to develop and produce evidence-based BCC packages under a multi-level media campaign to ensure effective, integrated BCC implementation through mass media and facility and community level interventions. The integrated project developed BCC strategies and tools like the Social and Behavior Change Communication Strategy and the Community Mobilization Strategy. The following key mass media activities were conducted:

i) ***Moyo ndi Mpamba* Campaign:** Informed and guided by the BCC strategy that was developed during the previous year, PMI supported the designing of a central, integrated

BCC campaign platform — *Moyo ndi Mpamba, Usamalireni*, "Life is Precious, Take care of it." The campaign provides a platform to tie together messages from the six focus health topics for the integrated platform (malaria; HIV/AIDS; maternal, neonatal and child health; family planning; water, sanitation, and hygiene; and nutrition). The MOH adopted the campaign as the brand identity for its health communication integration efforts. A *Moyo ndi Mpamba* album and music video was launched on radio and TV stations; 150 Moyo ndi *Mpamba* Music for Life albums were distributed to 15 radio stations, Support for Service Delivery Integration (SSDI) project partners and selected entertainment venues.

ii) **Malaria-specific messaging:** Aired a total of 860 radio spots, which were produced in collaboration with the NMCP and the Health Education Section, promoting use of ITNs, prompt care seeking, prompt diagnosis with RDTs and appropriate treatment. These messages were broadcast in the most widely spoken languages on the three national and most of the community radio stations; the radio spots reached approximately a quarter of the country's population.[12] In addition, 2,100 facility posters reminding health workers to perform RDT before treatment were distributed to health facilities across the country.

iii) *Cheni cheni ncheti (CCN)* **radio program:** Literally translated as "which is which?" CCN is a community-driven reality radio program focusing on key health issues in the community. Broadcasted on 12 programs on 15 radio stations, CCN has gained tremendous followership among rural communities, with an estimated reach of about 34 percent of the population listening to it twice a week[13] and community members regularly participating through SMS messages. The program has received over 3,200 feedback SMSs.

iv) **Community Mobilization Support:** With PMI support, partners conducted a three-day technical review meeting with all community mobilization Zonal Coordinators to review the implementation of the Community Action Cycle. Partners provided technical support on community mobilization to non-governmental organization sub-grantees, District Health Promotion Sub-committees, Community Mobilization district level trainers, Community Mobilization team members and Community Action Groups in the 15 SSDI focus districts where community mobilization is implemented. Partners conducted joint supervision visits with Health Education Services officials in Nkhotakota, Kasungu, Machinga and Mangochi districts to showcase the community mobilization activities in the districts.

v) **Media partnership:** The integrated project continued to build the capacity of key national-level institutional partners and district-level partners in 15 districts to ensure effective BCC strategic planning and delivery through on-going technical assistance and monitoring. The media is a crucial partner in promoting malaria prevention and control efforts and can provide a strong platform for advocacy with decision makers, as well as for changing attitudes and norms in the general population. However, airtime and print space are expensive and difficult to sustain in Malawi. *Media for Life* is an innovation for forging a mutually beneficial partnership between the health sector and the media with minimal costs to the MOH and the media partners. The integrated project supported the MOH through Health Education Services to conduct a Media for Life Conference. As part of the Media for Life Conference, four media houses signed a memorandum of understanding (MOUs) with the MOH. The MOUs are aimed at enhancing mutual contribution of media institutions and MOH in health promotion efforts.

---

[12] Based on SSDI baseline estimates through Zodiak, MBC 1 and MBC 2 radios only in the 15 SSDI districts

[13] 34 percent listen to it twice a week, according to SSDI-Communication baseline, 2012

Although the country has made significant strides, more progress is needed. The MIS 2014 shows that some malaria prevention behaviors, like IPTp2 uptake, is stagnant around 60 percent despite Malawi being the first country in sub-Saharan African to attain high levels of IPTp2 coverage. Similarly, prompt care seeking among under-five children still remains sub-optimal. These challenges represent opportunities to intensify community and health provider messaging to improve uptake of these interventions.

The GoM has recently changed its policy for treatment of severe malaria cases at community level to recommend diagnosis with RDTs and pre-referral treatment with rectal artesunate. To achieve optimal implementation of these interventions, PMI BCC activities have been planned to improve understanding of the acceptability of these interventions; this information will be used to foster increased utilization and demand of the new interventions.

Plans and justification
PMI plans to support an integrated BCC approach at the national level and at the community level in ten focus districts with ITN, IPTp, and case management messaging. National level efforts will focus on advocacy, mass media communication, and materials development, while community level efforts will focus on interpersonal and small group interventions.

Proposed activities with FY 2016 funding: ($1,758,000)
- Support for national-level BCC activities to improve uptake of malaria services and adoption of preventive and care-seeking behaviors; and technical assistance to community-based BCC activities. BCC is designed to promote prompt treatment of malaria, adherence to treatment, and early care-seeking behavior; to improve demand for ITN and increase use; and to improve IPTp uptake ($958,000);
- Community-based BCC activities to improve demand for services and uptake of core malaria prevention and control interventions. Small grants to community-based organizations to improve uptake of malaria services, adoption of preventive and care-seeking behaviors, and enhance civic engagement in oversight and accountability for health services ($800,000); and
- Support community based organizations to engage school-aged children and out-of-school adolescents to improve uptake of malaria prevention interventions at community level in Machinga and Mchinji districts; this includes promotion of ITN use among adolescents to cultivate a "net utilization culture" and promote ITN care and repair. ($0 - partner fully funded using previous years funds).

7. Monitoring and evaluation

NMCP/PMI objectives
The 2011-2016 Malaria Strategic Plan calls for strengthening of surveillance, monitoring and evaluation systems through routine health management information systems, malaria-specific surveillance and special surveys to gather entomologic, epidemiologic, and coverage indicator data. This plan follows RBM M&E guidance to provide a comprehensive framework for obtaining reliable and consistent data in order to assess progress toward the achievement of universal coverage of malaria interventions and the reduction of disease burden. PMI provides targeted programmatic and technical support to the NMCP, HTSS, and CMED to support

improvements to surveillance, monitoring and evaluation systems and enhance the coordination of GoM efforts.

Progress since PMI was launched
National household surveys

The UNICEF-funded 2006 MICS provides the baseline data for PMI's program. Although it collected information on net ownership and usage, as well as IPTp uptake, it did not include biomarker data. The NMCP, with assistance from the Malaria Control and Evaluation Partnership in Africa, completed Malawi's first MIS in April 2010. This survey documented increases in household net ownership, net usage in vulnerable groups, and uptake of IPTp. Nevertheless, high parasitemia (~43%) was noted. PMI provided support to the 2010 DHS, which provided district-level estimates of under-five mortality and malaria indicators. With FY 2012 funding, PMI supported the second MIS in Malawi. Please see the strategy section *Progress on indicators to date* for more detail.

Health facility and other surveys

Health facility surveys: With FY 2010 and FY 2011 funding, PMI supported nationally representative health facility surveys to assess the quality of case management for uncomplicated malaria in outpatient facilities and severe malaria in tertiary care facilities. Results from the outpatient facility evaluation showed poor provider adherence to microscopy results. (This survey was conducted prior to the roll-out of RDTs in Malawi.) Only two-thirds of patients with uncomplicated malaria confirmed by microscopy received an ACT and 31% of patients without malaria were inappropriately treated with an ACT. Results from the tertiary care facility evaluation identified limited availability of medications and diagnostic supplies, as well as knowledge gaps among health workers, as key obstacles to providing quality care for patients with severe malaria. The case fatality ratio among patients admitted with suspected or confirmed malaria was 2.15% (95% CI 0.79-3.52) in patients of all ages.

End-use verification surveys: PMI began supporting end-use verification surveys with FY 2011 funds. Initial surveys identified high percentages of facilities reporting stockouts: 38 to 55 percent of facilities with stockouts of three or more days across each AL presentation and approximately 75 percent of facilities with stockouts of SP. As reporting through the logistics management information system was incomplete and inconsistent, the end-use verification surveys have become an essential tool to help guide and improve inventory management at the health facility level.

The 2013-14 SPA was a census of all formal sector health facilities in Malawi. Please see *Strategy: Other relevant evidence on progress* for a summary of results.

Malaria surveillance and routine systems

PMI supported health facility surveillance via sentinel sites in Malawi from FY 2007 through FY 2010. However, PMI discontinued this support in FY 2011, based on an evaluation that found a key indicator for data quality — the proportion of suspect malaria cases that were laboratory confirmed — remained low.

The HMIS has been the primary system for monitoring the implementation of services and collecting disease surveillance data for the MOH. The HMIS collects and reports data on more than 70 core indicators, including outpatient malaria cases and inpatient malaria deaths. However, reporting of malaria cases through HMIS has been incomplete and inconsistent and has often lacked parasitological confirmation. In an attempt to improve system performance, the MOH began to transition the HMIS platform from DHIS to DHIS 2 in 2009. The DHIS 2 is a web-based system for capturing data at district level; HMIS relies on paper-based reporting at health facility level. While the MOH was overhauling the HMIS, the NMCP was granted authority to develop a parallel reporting system for malaria surveillance in 2011. PMI supported this activity through training of district health management teams in the parallel system surveillance forms and mentoring visits from the NMCP monitoring and evaluation officers. With support from PMI and other partners, the NMCP worked with the CMED to ensure that appropriate malaria indicators (including commodity indicators) were included in the DHIS 2 malaria-specific platform, enabling subsequent reintegration of the malaria parallel surveillance system with HMIS in 2013.

With FY 2013 funding, PMI supported the incorporation of malaria-specific data fields into an electronic medical records system, designed to provide patient-level malaria data at selected facilities and link clinical, laboratory and pharmacy data.

Therapeutic efficacy monitoring

Malawi has monitored the efficacy of its first (AL) and second-line (ASAQ) antimalarial drugs through *in vivo* drug efficacy studies. The first TES was conducted in six sites (PMI and GoM contributed funds); data were collected in 2011. This TES also included dihydroartemisinin-piperaquine, a potential future drug for Malawi. PCR-corrected cure rates at Day 28 were greater than 90 percent with all drugs. These results suggested that all three medications remained efficacious and were consistent with the findings from five additional sites monitored during the same time period under a GoM-funded study. No change in policy was recommended based on these data.

Entomological monitoring

Please see the IRS section for details of entomological monitoring.

Impact evaluation

With funding and support from PMI and the RBM partnership, Malawi completed the *Progress and Impact Series* report, which was disseminated in April 2013. Key findings include a 41 percent reduction in under-five mortality from 188 to 112 deaths per 1000 live births over the period 1996-2000 and 2006-2010. Modeling estimated that approximately 21,600 deaths among children under five years of age were prevented by malaria control interventions.

Progress during the last 12-18 months
National household surveys
With FY 2013 funding, PMI provided partial support and technical assistance to the third MIS in Malawi. The 2014 MIS was conducted during May-June 2014 and final results were disseminated in March 2015. A second MICS was also conducted during the first half of 2014 with support from UNICEF. At the time of writing, the key findings have been released but the full report is still pending. Please see *Strategy, section 8: Progress on indicators to date* for a summary of results from these national household surveys.

Health facility and other surveys

End-use verification surveys

In collaboration with the NMCP, two rounds of end-use verification survey field visits were completed in the past year. For these rounds, the percentage of facilities reporting stockouts of three or more days of first line ACTs and RDTs were substantially higher than those noted in previous EUVs (range: 15-42%). Overstocking of facilities (i.e., greater than 3-months supply) with ACTs and RDTs remained an issue. PMI also funded and provided technical assistance for a large-scale evaluation designed to assess the reasons for the imbalances between ACT/RDT consumption and morbidity reporting. This evaluation collected essentially all of the data elements normally included in an EUV exercise, as well as additional information required to understand the underlying causes of the imbalances, and was conducted in place of one of the planned EUV activities.

Malaria surveillance and routine systems

PMI continued to support improvements to the HMIS system, including data collection at the health facility level and timely and complete data entry into HMIS using DHIS 2 at the district level. The GoM is increasingly concerned about the quality of routine monitoring and surveillance data and CMED, with support from PMI and other partners, has developed a strategy to improve Malawi's overall health information system. Efforts are underway to streamline the core and program-specific indicators collected. PMI provided technical support to the implementation of this strategy to improve the overall system and ensure appropriate inclusion and collection of malaria data. Under this strategy, DHIS 2 will be the central data platform for the MOH. Currently, DHIS 2 is being used for routine data collection at the district level in all 29 districts in Malawi. Reporting from the community and facility levels to the district level is still paper-based. Overall, reporting rates for both the integrated HMIS reporting form and malaria-specific reporting form have improved over the last several years. In 2014, the reporting rates were 96% and 67%, respectively; however, considerable improvements in timeliness, completeness and data quality still are needed.

The CMED has developed a longer-term strategy for the overall health information system and plans to use DHIS 2 as the central repository for information on all key health indicators. The existing parallel systems either will be absorbed into DHIS 2 or linked. Furthermore, there are plans to link the electronic LMIS with DHIS 2 to improve Malawi's ability to compare morbidity and commodity consumption data. In addition to these structural changes to the system, CMED has undertaken a review of HMIS indicators and PMI has worked closely with

CMED, NMCP, Health Technical Support Services Unit, and other partners to select appropriate indicators and ensure that the appropriate tools are available to collect the data needed.

Therapeutic efficacy monitoring

In 2014, PMI supported additional therapeutic efficacy monitoring for AL and ASAQ in three sites, one in each region of Malawi. This study demonstrated excellent efficacy of both AL and ASAQ, with PCR-corrected survival rates at Day 28 of 99.3% (95% CI: 98.3–100%) for AL, with 98-100% efficacy in each region, and 99% (95% CI: 97.2–100%) for ASAQ, supporting the continued use of these drugs as first and second line therapies. No policy change was recommended.

Entomological monitoring

Entomologic and insecticide resistance monitoring

PMI continued to provide support for entomologic and insecticide resistance monitoring. The NMCP, with support from PMI and input from stakeholders, conducted a review of existing entomological monitoring data and developed an evidenced-based vector control strategy that will guide future entomological monitoring. The implementation plan for this strategy is currently under development.

Table 8: Monitoring and Evaluation Activity Summary Table

Data source	Survey activities	2006	2007	2008	2009	2010	2011	2012	2013	2014	2015	2016	2017
Household surveys	Multiple indicator cluster survey	X*†								X*			
	Demographic and Health Survey					X§					X		
	Malaria Indicator Survey					X¶		X¶		X¶		X	
	Subnational anemia and parasitemia survey	X	X	X									
Health facility and other surveys	Health facility and related surveys				X**		X††	X††					
	Service provision assessment								X§§				
	End-use verification survey						X	X	X	X	X	X	X
Malaria surveillance and routine system support	Sentinel surveillance		X	X	X	X							
	Support to malaria surveillance system						X	X	X	X¶¶	X	X	
	Support to HMIS		X	X	X	X	X	X	X	X	X	X	X
Therapeutic	In vivo efficacy testing						X			X			
Entomology			X	X	X	X	X	X	X	X	X	X	X
Other data sources	Malaria impact evaluation								X				

59

* Not PMI funded

†MICS conducted by UNICEF. Report for 2006 available at http://www.childinfo.org/files/MICS3_Malawi_FinalReport_2006_eng.pdf. Report for 2014 pending.

§ 2010 DHS available at http://www.measuredhs.com/what-we-do/survey/survey-display-333.cfm

¶ 2010 MIS conducted with technical assistance from the Malaria Control and Evaluation Partnership in Africa (MACEPA), report available at http://www.givewell.org/files/DWDA%202009/AMF/Malawi_MIS_2010_Final.pdf. 2012 MIS conducted by ICF-MACRO, data and report available at http://www.measuredhs.com/what-we-do/survey/survey-display-432.cfm. 2014 MIS supported by the Global Fund with technical assistance provided by PMI and ICF-MACRO.

**Evaluation of IMCI program

††The health facility survey in 2011 focused on the management of uncomplicated malaria. The subsequent health facility survey in 2012 focused on the management of severe malaria.

§§SPA was conducted during the last two quarters of 2013 and first half of 2014

¶¶ Additional funding provided for one-time support to develop and incorporate malaria-specific indicators into an electronic medical records data management system.

Plans and justification
National household surveys

Since 2010, there have been unusually frequent national household surveys undertaken in Malawi: five national surveys (2010 DHS, 2010 MIS, 2012 MIS, 2014 MICS, and 2014 MIS), and plans to conduct at least two more in the coming years (2015 DHS and 2016 MIS). This situation is due to multiple and complex factors, including: poor coordination between implementation of program activities and survey timing (e.g., 2012 ITN mass distribution campaign delayed so effect on ITN ownership was not captured in 2012 MIS); various programs requiring information not captured in a planned national survey (e.g., NMCP desiring wet season parasitemia data not captured in the DHS); and poor coordination between programs and stakeholders (e.g., 2014 MICS planned the year before 2015 DHS). PMI continues to discuss its concern about the excessive number of national household surveys with the MOH, NMCP, USAID Mission, and other donor partners.

Because ITN ownership and usage were not assessed after the 2012 ITN mass distribution campaign, it is critical to assess these indicators after the planned 2015 ITN mass distribution campaign. PMI is providing partial support to the planned 2015 DHS; the primary indicators needed from this survey are ITN ownership and usage. Originally, data collection for the 2015 DHS was expected to occur in mid to late 2015, following the planned ITN mass distribution campaign. However, both the DHS and the ITN campaign have had significant delays and it is unclear whether the ITN distribution will occur prior to the DHS. It is also unclear whether the DHS will be conducted in calendar year 2015. To complicate matters further, Malawi is scheduled to conduct its fourth MIS in calendar year 2016 with support from PMI. At the time of writing, PMI plans to support the planned 2015 DHS. If this survey is conducted in 2015 prior to the ITN mass distribution campaign, PMI will support the 2016 MIS to assess ITN ownership and use following the campaign. If the DHS does not occur until early 2016, PMI will advocate for inclusion of parasitemia in the DHS module and postponement of the planned 2016 MIS. PMI has no plans to support national household surveys with FY 2016 funds.

Health facility and other surveys

There are no plans for additional health facility surveys or SPA at this time. PMI plans to continue to support to quarterly end-use verification surveys.

Malaria surveillance and routine systems

PMI has been providing support to oversee data collection at the health facility level and data entry into DHIS 2. However, additional support is required to build on the improvements made to the HMIS. PMI currently provides technical assistance to health information systems at the central level and is working to arrange further support to CMED using FY 2014 and FY 2015 funding. PMI will continue to support efforts to improve routine data collection and build HMIS capacity at all levels of the health system using FY 2016 funding.

Therapeutic efficacy monitoring

Malawi conducts a TES in three to four sites approximately every two years and plans to conduct a TES in 2016 with Global Fund support.[14] As a result, PMI has reprogrammed the FY 2015 funding for this TES and has not included funding for this activity in FY 2016.

Entomological monitoring

PMI plans to continue support for entomologic and insecticide resistance monitoring to provide data for evidence-based decision-making for vector control interventions. Please see the IRS section for details of entomological monitoring.

Proposed activities with FY 2016 funding: **($1,289,000)**
PMI plans to continue to support strengthening of routine health management information systems and malaria-specific surveillance and special surveys to gather entomologic, epidemiologic, and coverage indicator data. For district-level activities conducted in the ten PMI focus districts, PMI will work closely with CMED, HTSS, NMCP and other malaria partners to ensure that these activities are in-line with the priorities of the GoM, support national level initiatives, and are coordinated with the activities of other partners working in the non-focus districts. PMI will also provide continued support for ITN durability monitoring following the 2015 mass campaign. Specifically, with FY 2016 funding, PMI will:

- Support quarterly end-use verification surveys to assess the availability of malaria commodities at health facilities ($200,000);
- Continue efforts to strengthen routine data collection through training and supervision at the district and health facility level in targeted districts ($300,000);
- Continue to improve CMED's management and implementation of national routine HMIS, including improved oversight and outreach to district staff and better coordination of the HMIS at the district and central levels ($300,000);
- Continue support for entomologic monitoring with routine surveys of vector density and insecticide resistance testing of mosquitoes in selected districts ($350,000);
- Continue support for ITN durability monitoring following the 2015 mass distribution campaign ($100,000).
- Technical assistance for entomological monitoring ($29,000);
- Technical assistance for M&E ($10,000).

8. Operational research

NMCP/PMI objectives

The 2011-2015 Malaria Strategic Plan calls for strengthening operational research through the support of local capacity building and the creation of stronger coordination between NMCP and researchers to harmonize and prioritize operational research efforts. PMI-funded operational research has provided important data for decision-making, including studies measuring the

---

[14] Malawi policy is to conduct a TES every two years. However, there was a three year interval between the most recent studies conducted in 2011 and 2014.

durability of long-lasting ITNs, the impact of IRS, the effectiveness of the IPTp strategy, the quality of health facility case management practices for uncomplicated and severe malaria, the ability of patients to complete recommended first-line treatment for malaria, the distribution of potentially drug-resistant parasites and mosquitoes and the effectiveness of ITNs in an area with significant pyrethroid resistance.

Table 9: Operational Research supported by PMI Malawi

Completed OR Studies			
Title	**Start Date**	**End Date**	**Funding Level (US$)**
IPTp effectiveness monitoring	2008	2012	40,000
SP drug resistance markers in pregnant women	2008	2012	0
Health facility surveys: management of uncomplicated and severe malaria	2008	2012	330,000
Pilot study of intermittent preventative treatments for infants	2008	completed	150,000
Patient adherence to first-line treatment of malaria	2009	2011	140,000
Pilot study of community ACT use through HSAs	2010	completed	200,000
Ongoing and Planned OR Studies			
Title	**Start Date**	**End Date**	**Funding Level (US$)**
IPTp effectiveness monitoring in areas with high levels of resistance	2015	2017	275,000
SP drug resistance markers in pregnant women	2015	2017	75,000
Evaluation of mobile-telephone text messaging intervention to improve health worker performance	2014	2016	520,000

Progress since the launch of PMI

Since PMI began, operational research investments in Malawi have produced important findings that have shaped NMCP and PMI policy and programs. The peer-reviewed publications from PMI-supported OR in partnership with the NMCP include:

- Gutman J, Mwandama D, Wiegand RE, Abdallah J, Iriemenam NC, Shi YP, Mathanga DP, Skarbinski J. (2015) In vivo efficacy of sulphadoxine-pyrimethamine for the treatment of asymptomatic parasitaemia in pregnant women in Machinga District, Malawi. *Malar J.* 2015;14:197.
- Gutman J, Kalilani L, Taylor S, Zhou Z, Wiegand RE, Thwai KL, Mwandama D, Khairallah C, Madanitsa M, Chaluluka E, Dzinjalamala F, Ali D, Mathanga DP, Skarbinski J, Shi YP, Meshnick S, Ter Kuile FO. (2015) The A581G Mutation in the Gene Encoding Plasmodium falciparum Dihydropteroate Synthetase Reduces the

Effectiveness of Sulfadoxine-Pyrimethamine Preventive Therapy in Malawian Pregnant Women. *J Infect Dis.* 2015;211(12):1997-2005.

- Wong J, Shah MP, Mwandama D, Gimnig JE, Lindblade KA, Mathanga DP. (2015) Home visits to assess the reliability of caregiver-reported use of insecticide-treated bednets by children in Machinga District, Malawi. *Am J Trop Med Hyg.* 92(4):825-7.

- Lindblade KA, Mwandama D, Mzilahowa T, Steinhardt L, Gimnig J, Shah M, Bauleni A, Wong J, Wiegand R, Howell P, Zoya J, Chiphwanya J, Mathanga DP. (2015) A cohort study of the effectiveness of insecticide-treated bed nets to prevent malaria in an area of moderate pyrethroid resistance, Malawi. *Malar J.* 14:31.

- Zhou Z, Mitchell RM, Gutman J, Wiegand RE, Mwandama DA, Mathanga DP, Skarbinski J, Shi YP. (2014) Pooled PCR testing strategy and prevalence estimation of submicroscopic infections using Bayesian latent class models in pregnant women receiving intermittent preventive treatment at Machinga District Hospital, Malawi, 2010. *Malar J.* 2014;13:509.

- Taylor SM, Parobek CM, DeConti DK, Kayentao K, Coulibaly SO, Greenwood BM, Tagbor H, Williams J, Bojang K, Njie F, Desai M, Kariuki S, Gutman J, Mathanga DP, Mårtensson A, Ngasala B, Conrad MD, Rosenthal PJ, Tshefu AK, Moormann AM, Vulule JM, Doumbo OK, Ter Kuile FO, Meshnick SR, Bailey JA, Juliano JJ. (2015) Absence of putative artemisinin resistance mutations among Plasmodium falciparum in Sub-Saharan Africa: a molecular epidemiologic study. *J Infect Dis.* 211(5):680-8.

- LC Steinhardt, J Chinkhumba, A Wolkon, M Luka, M Luhanga, J Sande, J Oyugi, D Ali, DP Mathanga, J Skarbinski (2014). Patient-, health worker-, and health facility-level determinants of correct malaria case management at publicly funded health facilities in Malawi: results from a nationally representative health facility survey. *Malaria Journal* 13:64e.

- LC Steinhardt, J Chinkhumba, A Wolkon, M Luka, M Luhanga, J Sande, J Oyugi, D Ali, DP Mathanga, J Skarbinski (2014). Quality of malaria case management in Malawi: results from a nationally representative health facility survey. *PLoS One* 9(2):e89050.

- J Gutman, D Mwandama, RE Wiegand, D Ali, DP Mathanga, J Skarbinski (2013). Effectiveness of intermittent preventive treatment with sulfadoxine-pyrimethamine during pregnancy on maternal and birth outcomes in Machinga District, Malawi. *Journal of Infectious Diseases* 208(6):907-16.

- C Hershey, D Ali, L Florey, A Bennett, M Luhanga, J Oyugi, Y Ye, G Jenda, C Nielsen, SR Salgado, DP Mathanga, A Bhattarai (2013). Secondary analysis of national and subnational survey data to evaluate the impact of the scale up of malaria control interventions in Malawi, 2000--2010 [meeting abstract]. *Lancet* 381(S2):S60.

- J Skarbinski, D Mwandama, A Wolkon, M Luka, J Jafali, A Smith, T Mzilahowa, J Gimnig, C Campbell, J Chiphwanya, D Ali, DP Mathanga (2012). Impact of indoor residual spraying with lambda-cyhalothrin on malaria parasitemia and anemia prevalence among children less than five years of age in an area of intense, year-round transmission in Malawi. *American Journal of Tropical Medicine and Hygiene* 86(6):997-1004.

- J Chinkhumba, M Nyanda, J Skarbinski, DP Mathanga (2012). Performance of two malaria rapid diagnostic tests in febrile adult patients with and without human immunodeficiency virus-1 infection in Blantyre, Malawi. *American Journal of Tropical Medicine and Hygiene* 86(2):199-201.

- PS Larson, DP Mathanga, CH Campbell Jr, ML Wilson (2012). Distance to health services influences insecticide-treated net possession and use among 6 to 59 month-old children in Malawi. *Malaria Journal* 11:18e.
- KE Mace, D Mwandama, J Jafali, M Luka, SJ Filler, J Sande, D Ali, SP Kachur, DP Mathanga, J Skarbinski (2011). Adherence to treatment with artemether-lumefantrine for uncomplicated malaria in rural Malawi. *Clinical Infectious Diseases* 53(8):772-9.
- J Skarbinski, D Mwandama, M Luka, J Jafali, A Wolkon, D Townes, C Campbell, J Zoya, D Ali, DP Mathanga (2011). Impact of health facility-based insecticide treated bednet distribution in Malawi: progress and challenges towards achieving universal coverage. *PLoS One* 6(7):e21995.
- J Chinkhumba, J Skarbinski, B Chilima, C Campbell, V Ewing, M San Joaquin, M Sande, D Ali, D Mathanga (2010). Comparative field performance and adherence to test results of four malaria rapid diagnostic tests among febrile patients more than five years of age in Blantyre, Malawi. *Malaria Journal* 9:209e.
- DP Mathanga, CH Campbell Jr, J Vanden Eng, A Wolkon, RN Bronzan, GJ Malenga, D Ali, M Desai (2010). Comparison of anaemia and parasitaemia as indicators of malaria control in household and EPI-health facility surveys. *Malaria Journal* 9:107e.
- AI Chibwana, DP Mathanga, J Chinkhumba, CH Campbell Jr (2009). Socio-cultural predictors of health-seeking behavior for febrile under-five children in Mwanza-Neno District, Malawi. *Malaria Journal* 8:219e.
- DP Mathanga, ET Luman, CH Campbell Jr, C Silwimba, G Malenga (2009). Integration of insecticide-treated net distribution into routine immunization services in Malawi: a pilot study. *Tropical Medicine and International Health* 14(7):792-801.

Progress in the last 12-18 months

The PMI-funded evaluation of mobile-telephone text messaging to improve health worker performance was initiated in early 2015. A baseline survey of health worker case management practices was conducted, followed by a stakeholder workshop to design the content of the messages. Delivery of the messages is currently ongoing, with end-line surveys planned for the November 2015 and May 2016 to assess the impact of the intervention. In 2015, using reprogrammed FY 2012 funds, PMI will continue to monitor the levels of SP resistance (using samples collected during the 2014 TES) and will support a repeat evaluation of the effectiveness of IPTp focusing on the effect of the sextuple (dhps581) mutation, which is associated with extremely high levels of resistance. This evaluation was delayed and implementation is planned for July-September 2015. In addition, with FY 2014 funding, PMI is providing support to the NMCP to develop a research agenda and data dissemination platform to better coordinate and share research among partners in Malawi (see Health Systems Strengthening and Capacity Building section).

Plans and justification

The research focus will be to complete the ongoing cell phone messaging evaluation (funded with FY 2013 funds), and a study to assess the efficacy of IPTp with dihydroartemisin-piperaquine (DP) compared to SP (planned to begin in early 2016 using FY 2013 funds).

As highlighted in the *Malaria in Pregnancy* section, IPTp coverage goals have yet to be met despite two decades of IPTp implementation in Malawi. There are still systemic barriers to seeking ANC in the first trimester and to receiving three or more doses of IPTp during pregnancy. To address this, PMI Malawi plans to initiate an evaluation of the effect of community delivery of IPTp-SP on IPTp uptake and ANC attendance. The specific approach for this study will be determined through consultations with the NMCP and the Reproductive Health Directorate of the MOH.

Proposed activities with FY 2016 funding: **($390,000)**

- Study of the effectiveness of IPTp-DP versus IPTp-SP ($150,000, in addition to $250,000 reprogrammed from FY 2013 funds)
- Study to determine effect of community delivery of IPTp on IPTp uptake and ANC attendance ($200,000)
- Technical assistance for operational research ($40,000 for 4 TDYs)

9. Staffing and administration

Two health professionals serve as resident advisors to oversee PMI in Malawi, one representing CDC and one representing USAID. In addition, three Foreign Service Nationals (FSNs) work as part of the PMI team. All PMI staff members are part of a single interagency team led by the USAID Mission Director or his/her designee in country. The PMI team shares responsibility for development and implementation of PMI strategies and work plans, coordination with national authorities, managing collaborating agencies and supervising day-to-day activities. Candidates for resident advisor positions (whether initial hires or replacements) will be evaluated and/or interviewed jointly by USAID and CDC, and both agencies will be involved in hiring decisions, with the final decision made by the individual agency.

The PMI professional staff work together to oversee all technical and administrative aspects of the PMI, including finalizing details of the project design, implementing malaria prevention and treatment activities, monitoring and evaluation of outcomes and impact, reporting of results, and providing guidance to PMI partners.

The PMI lead in country is the USAID Mission Director. The day-to-day lead for PMI is delegated to the USAID Health Office Director and thus the two PMI resident advisors, one from USAID and one from CDC, report to the USAID Health Office Director for day-to-day leadership, and work together as a part of a single interagency team. The technical expertise housed in Atlanta and Washington guides PMI programmatic efforts.

The two PMI resident advisors are based within the USAID health office and are expected to spend approximately half their time sitting with and providing technical assistance to the national malaria control program and partners.

Locally-hired staff to support PMI activities either in Ministries or in USAID will be approved by the USAID Mission Director.

Proposed activities with FY 2016 funding: **($1,975,000)**
- Support to CDC for staffing ($575,000);
- Support to USAID for staffing ($960,000);
- Support to USAID for administration and technical oversight ($440,000)

Table 1: Budget Breakdown by Mechanism

President's Malaria Initiative – MALAWI

Planned Malaria Obligations for FY 2016

Mechanism	Geographic Area	Activity	Budget ($)	%
GHSC	Nationwide	Procurement of ITNs, SP and ANC supplies, RDTs and ancillary supplies, and ACTs; management, oversight, and delivery of procured commodities; improve facility-level commodities storage capacity	11,743,000	53%
IRS 2 TO6	Select Districts	Technical assistance to NMCP in support of IRS activities	250,000	1%
GEMS II	Select Districts	Environmental compliance support to NMCP for IRS activities	50,000	0%
TBD-Service Delivery Partner	10 Focus Districts	Strengthening MIP and case management services; support to district health offices, district malaria coordinators, and zonal health offices; support for community-based SBCC; strengthening routine HMIS at facility level	3,125,000	14%
Malaria Care	10 Focus Districts	Strengthening diagnostic services at facility level	750,000	3%
TBD-Supply Chain TA Partner	Central Level	Technical assistance to GoM to improve management, oversight, and accountability for supply chain and logistics management; support for quarterly EUVs	1,200,000	5%

TBD-Systems Partner	Central Level	Support to NMCP for basic operational functioning, technical working group and research dissemination meetings, short courses and regional or international meetings; support to CMED to build capacity for malaria data collection, management, analysis, and use; support central-level HMIS	770,000	4%
World Learning	Central Level	Support pre-service training for 48 pharmacy assistants; support for pre-service training curricula revision	250,000	1%
Peace Corps	Nationwide	Support three Peace Corps volunteers to work with the NMCP and coordinate Peace Corps activities for malaria	40,000	0%
TBD-Communications Partner	10 Focus Districts	Support for national-level BCC activities to improve uptake of malaria services and adoption of preventive and care-seeking behaviors; technical assistance to community-based BCC activities	958,000	4%
CDC/MAC	Select Districts	IPTp DP vs. SP study	150,000	3%
TBD	Select Districts	ITN durability monitoring, entomological monitoring, Study to determine effect of community delivery of IPTp on IPTp uptake and ANC attendance	650,000	1%
CDC		Entomology, OR, and M&E TDYs; in-country staffing	664,000	3%
USAID		In-country staffing; PD&L	1,400,000	6%
Total			**22,000,000**	**100%***

* Partner percentages do not total 100% due to rounding error.

Table 2: Budget Breakdown by Activity

President's Malaria Initiative – MALAWI

Planned Malaria Obligations for FY 2016

Proposed Activity	Mechanism	Budget		Geographic Area	Description
		Total $	Commodity $		
PREVENTIVE ACTIVITIES					
Insecticide-treated Nets					
Procurement of ITNs for routine distribution	GHSC	2,856,000	2,856,000	Nationwide	Procure approximately 800,000 ITNs for continuous distribution through routine channels
Support for PMI parallel supply chain	GHSC	800,000		Nationwide	Support management, oversight, and distribution of PMI-procured ITNs to health facilities for routine distribution. Provide technical assistance for ITN quantification and distribution planning, monitoring of ITN distribution, and supportive supervision of ANC and EPI staff.
SUBTOTAL ITNs		3,656,000	2,856,000		
Indoor Residual Spraying					
Technical assistance to NMCP in support of IRS activities	IRS 2 TO6	250,000		Select districts	Technical assistance to NMCP in support of IRS activities
Environmental compliance support to NMCP for IRS	GEMS II	50,000		Select districts	Environmental compliance support to NMCP for IRS

70

activities					activities
Technical support for IVM implementation plan	CDC		10,000		One TDY to provide technical assistance in developing the Integrated Vector Management implementation plan
SUBTOTAL IRS			310,000	0	
Malaria in Pregnancy					
Procurement of SP	GHSC	Nationwide	300,000	300,000	Procure approximately 2,000,000 treatment courses of SP for IPTp
Procurement of supplies for directly observed therapy for IPTp	GHSC	Nationwide	50,000	50,000	Procure ANC supplies (cups, water buckets) to help improve IPTp uptake
Strengthening malaria in pregnancy services through support for focused ANC	TBD- Service delivery partner	10 focus districts	400,000		Support proper implementation of IPTp and ITN distribution in selected districts, including supportive supervision and mentorship
Subtotal Malaria in Pregnancy			750,000	350,000	
SUBTOTAL PREVENTIVE			4,716,000	3,206,000	
CASE MANAGEMENT					
Diagnosis and Treatment					
Procurement of RDTs	GHSC	Nationwide	1,517,000	1,517,000	Procure approximately 4.1 million RDTs for use in facilities and village health clinics
Procurement of ACTs	GHSC	Nationwide	4,270,000	4,270,000	Procure approximately 3.5 million courses of first-line ACTs for use in health facilities and village health clinics

Activity	Description	Location			Partner
Procurement of ancillary diagnostic supplies	Procure sufficient ancillary supplies (gloves, sharps boxes) for RDT implementation	Nationwide	150,000	150,000	GHSC
Strengthen facility and community-based case management services	Technical assistance and operational support to improve facility and community-based case management services and systems	10 focus districts		1,325,000	TBD- Service delivery partner
Support diagnostic services at facility and community levels	Strengthen diagnostic services to ensure appropriate use of RDTs and microscopy at facility and community levels	10 focus districts		750,000	MalariaCare
Subtotal Diagnosis and Treatment			**5,937,000**	**8,012,000**	
Pharmaceutical Management					
Technical assistance to strengthen the national supply chain system	Technical assistance to GoM to improve management, oversight, and accountability for supply chain and logistics management	Central level		1,000,000	TBD- Supply Chain TA partner
Support for PMI parallel supply chain	Support management, oversight, and distribution of PMI-procured commodities	Nationwide		1,500,000	GHSC
Subtotal Pharmaceutical Management				**2,500,000**	
SUBTOTAL CASE MANAGEMENT			**5,937,000**	**10,512,000**	
HEALTH SYSTEM STRENGTHENING / CAPACITY BUILDING					

Activity	Partner	Budget		Location	Description
Support to district malaria coordinators, district health offices, and zonal health offices	TBD - Service delivery partner	300,000		10 focus districts	Support key district health staff to conduct facility and community-level supportive supervision, mentorship, coaching, and assistance with data collection and reporting, as well as support to the zonal offices for improved supervision and oversight
Logistical and operational support to NMCP	TBD - Systems partner	240,000		Central level	Support to NMCP to hold technical working group and research dissemination meetings and support basic operational functioning
Support to NMCP for professional development and conferences	TBD - Systems partner	30,000		Central level	Support NMCP to participate in short courses and regional and international meetings to expand knowledge base
Support for MOH Central Monitoring and Evaluation Division	TBD - Systems partner	200,000		Central level	Support CMED to build capacity for malaria data collection, management, analysis, and use at all levels of the health system
Improve facility-level commodity storage capacity	GHSC	300,000		Select districts	Support for a limited number of pre-fabricated storage containers for health facilities
Support pre-service training of pharmacy assistants	World Learning	200,000		Central level	Support pre-service training for 48 pharmacy assistants (24 students per cohort in a 2-year program)

Activity	Partner	Location	Amount		Description
Revision of pre-service curricula	World Learning	Central level	50,000		Support to update pre-service curricula at training institutions to ensure health workers entering the workforce have received training on the current malaria guidelines and practices
Peace Corps	Peace Corps	Nationwide	40,000		Support three Peace Corps volunteers to work with the NMCP and coordinate Peace Corps activities for malaria and small project activities
SUBTOTAL HSS & CAPACITY BUILDING			**1,360,000**	0	
BEHAVIOR CHANGE COMMUNICATION					
Support for nationwide and community BCC activities	TBD Communications partner	Nationwide	958,000		Support for national-level BCC activities to improve uptake of malaria services and adoption of preventive and care-seeking behaviors; technical assistance to community-based BCC activities
Support for community-based SBCC activities	TBD Service delivery partner	10 focus districts	800,000		Small grants to community-based NGOs to improve uptake of malaria services, adoption of preventive and care-seeking behaviors, and enhance civic engagement in oversight and accountability for health services
SUBTOTAL BCC			**1,758,000**	0	
MONITORING AND EVALUATION					
End-use verification surveys	TBD- Supply Chain TA partner	Nationwide	200,000		Support for quarterly monitoring of PMI-procured commodities at community level

Activity	Description	Location	Cost (USD)	Funding Source
Strengthen routine HMIS at the district level	Continue efforts to strengthen routine data collection through training and supervision at the district and health facility level in targeted districts	10 focus districts	300,000	TBD - Service delivery partner
Strengthen routine HMIS at central level	Continue to support central level routine HMIS, including support to CMED	Central level	300,000	TBD - Systems partner
Entomological monitoring	Continue support for entomologic monitoring with routine surveys of vector density and insecticide resistance testing of mosquitoes in selected districts	Select districts	350,000	TBD
ITN durability monitoring	Continue to monitor ITN durability following the 2015 mass campaign	Select districts	100,000	TBD
Technical assistance for entomological monitoring	Two TDYs to provide technical assistance in entomological monitoring		29,000	CDC
Technical assistance for M&E	One TDY to provide technical assistance in M&E		10,000	CDC
SUBTOTAL M&E	0		**1,289,000**	
OPERATIONAL RESEARCH				
IPTp DP-SP study	Continued support for study of the effectiveness of IPTp-dihydroartemisinin-piperaquine versus IPTp-SP	Select districts	150,000	CDC/MAC
Study to determine effect of community delivery of IPTp on IPTp uptake and ANC attendance	Study to determine effect of community delivery of IPTp on IPTp uptake and ANC attendance	Select districts	200,000	TBD
Technical assistance for operational research	Four TDYs to provide technical assistance to ongoing operational research activities		40,000	CDC

SUBTOTAL OR			390,000	0
	IN-COUNTRY STAFFING AND ADMINISTRATION			
	CDC	575,000		
	USAID	1,400,000		
SUBTOTAL IN-COUNTRY STAFFING		1,975,000		0
GRAND TOTAL		22,000,000	9,143,000	

www.ingramcontent.com/pod-product-compliance
Lightning Source LLC
Chambersburg PA
CBHW081238280526
45787CB00006B/2712